Principles and Practices of Assessment

SAGE was founded in 1965 by Sara Miller McCune to support the dissemination of usable knowledge by publishing innovative and high-quality research and teaching content. Today, we publish over 900 journals, including those of more than 400 learned societies, more than 800 new books per year, and a growing range of library products including archives, data, case studies, reports, and video. SAGE remains majority-owned by our founder, and after Sara's lifetime will become owned by a charitable trust that secures our continued independence.

Los Angeles | London | New Delhi | Singapore | Washington DC

Principles and Practices of Assessment

A guide for assessors in the FE and skills sector

Ann Gravells

Los Angeles | London | New Delhi
Singapore | Washington DC

Third Edition

Learning Matters
An imprint of SAGE Publications Ltd
1 Oliver's Yard
55 City Road
London EC1Y 1SP

SAGE Publications Inc.
2455 Teller Road
Thousand Oaks, California 91320

SAGE Publications India Pvt Ltd
B 1/I 1 Mohan Cooperative Industrial Area
Mathura Road
New Delhi 110 044

SAGE Publications Asia-Pacific Pte Ltd
3 Church Street
#10-04 Samsung Hub
Singapore 049483

Editor: Amy Thornton
Development editor: Jennifer Clark
Copy editor: Kathryn Wolfendale
Proof reader: Brian McDowell
Production controller: Chris Marke
Project management: Deer Park Productions
Marketing manager: Catherine Slinn
Cover design: Wendy Scott
Typeset by: C&M Digitals (P) Ltd, Chennai, India
Printed by: CPI Group (UK) Ltd, Croydon, CR0 4YY

First published in 2009 by Learning Matters Ltd
Reprinted in 2009
Reprinted in 2010
Second edition published in 2011
Third edition published in 2016

Library of Congress Control Number: 2015951584

British Library Cataloguing in Publication Data

A catalogue record for this book is available from the
British Library.

ISBN 978-1-4739-3938-7 (pbk)
ISBN 978-1-4739-3937-0

At SAGE we take sustainability seriously. Most of our products are printed in the UK using FSC papers and boards.
When we print overseas we ensure sustainable papers are used as measured by the PREPS grading system.
We undertake an annual audit to monitor our sustainability.

CONTENTS

ACKNOWLEDGEMENTS

I would like to give a special thanks to the following people who have helped me with this edition of the book. They have freely given their time, knowledge and advice, resulting in some excellent contributions to the content in the book.

Alison Quilliam, Quality Manager, The Manchester College

Helen Marshall, Director, Helios People Development

Jacqueline Rayner, Teaching and Learning Coach, The Manchester College

Joan Willison, Quality Manager, Activ8 Learning

Jonathan White, Subject Librarian, University of Derby

Laura Lewis-Davies FRSA, Freelance Qualifications and Quality Assurance Consultant, Learning Manager at the Museum of Brands

Roisin Kelly, Skills Development Coordinator, NICVA

Sharron Carlill, Assistant Principal (Quality and Compliance), The White Rose Beauty Colleges

Susan Harrison, Customer Management Service Manager, North East Lincolnshire Council

Particular thanks go to readers of previous editions of this book who have taken the time to give valuable feedback, which has greatly assisted me when preparing this edition.

I would like to thank my Senior Commissioning Editor (Education) Amy Thornton, and my Development Editor Jennifer Clark for their continued support and guidance.

Every effort has been made to trace the copyright holders and to obtain their permission for the use of copyright material. The publisher and author will gladly receive any information enabling them to rectify any error or omission in subsequent editions.

Ann Gravells

www.anngravells.co.uk

Ann Gravells has been teaching and assessing in the further education and skills sector since 1983. She is a director of her own company, Ann Gravells Ltd, an educational consultancy based in East Yorkshire. She specialises in teaching, training, assessment and quality assurance for the further education and skills sector. Ann holds a Master's in Educational Management, a PGCE, a Degree in Education, and a City & Guilds Medal of Excellence for teaching. She is a Fellow of the Society for Education and Training, and holds QTLS status.

Ann creates resources for teachers and learners such as PowerPoints and handouts for the assessment, and teacher training qualifications. These are available via her website: www.anngravells.co.uk/resources

Ann has worked for several awarding organisations producing qualification guidance, policies and procedures, and carrying out quality assurance of teacher training qualifications.

She is currently a consultant to the University of Cambridge's Institute of Continuing Education, and to Training Qualifications UK (TQUK), the UK's fastest growing awarding organisation which specialises in Education and Training, Assessment and Quality Assurance qualifications.

The author welcomes any comments from readers; please contact her via her website: www.anngravells.co.uk or email: consult@anngravells.co.uk

Ann Gravells is the author of the following books (in alphabetical order). Details can be found on her website: www.anngravells.co.uk/books

Achieving your Assessment and Quality Assurance Units (TAQA)

Delivering Employability Skills in the Lifelong Learning Sector

Passing Assessments for the Award in Education and Training

Passing PTLLS Assessments

Preparing to Teach in the Lifelong Learning Sector

Principles and Practices of Assessment in the Lifelong Learning Sector

The Award in Education and Training

What is Teaching in the Lifelong Learning Sector?

She is co-author of:

Equality and Diversity in the Lifelong Learning Sector

Passing CTLLS Assessments

Planning and Enabling Learning in the Lifelong Learning Sector

The Best Vocational Trainer's Guide

The Certificate in Education and Training

Passing Assessments for the Certificate in Education and Training

She has edited:

Study Skills for PTLLS

INTRODUCTION

Congratulations on purchasing this book. Whether you are a new or an experienced assessor, this book will guide you through the terminology, principles and practices to enable you to become an assessor, improve your role and/or work towards a relevant assessment qualification if necessary. The book is also applicable to anyone taking assessment units which form part of the teacher training qualifications.

Your role as an assessor might differ depending upon the type of employment contract you have, for example, full time, part time, freelance or self-employed. As you work through the book, some aspects might therefore not apply to you.

This book was first published in 2009, with a second edition in 2011. Although the principles and practices of assessment remain the same, the assessment qualifications in the further education and skills sector have changed. Some aspects of this subject are also covered in my book *Achieving your Assessment and Quality Assurance Units (TAQA)* (2014).

For the purpose of future-proofing the book, on the examples of assessment documents within the chapters the year has not been added to the date. Assessors should add the year as well as the day and month to create a full audit trail.

Due to the terminology used throughout the further education and skills sector, you will find lots of acronyms within the book. A list of the most commonly used ones can be found in the Appendix.

The term *learner* is used during the book to denote anyone being assessed, who might not necessarily call themselves a learner, such as an employee or apprentice in the workplace. The term *assessor* is used for anyone who assesses; however, the assessor might also be a teacher, trainer, coach or mentor.

There are activities and examples within each chapter which will assist your understanding of assessment principles and practice. At the end of each section within the chapters is an extension activity to stretch and challenge your learning further. Completing the activities will help you put theory into practice.

Throughout the chapters there are examples of completed templates that could be used or adapted for assessment purposes. However, do check with the organisation you are assessing for, in case they have particular documents they require you to use.

At the end of each chapter is a list of relevant text books and websites enabling you to research topics further. As these are often revised and updated, some might become unavailable over time.

The index at the back of the book will help you quickly locate useful topics within the book.

> **Introduction**
>
> Assessment is a way of checking if learning has taken place. It enables you, as the assessor, to ascertain if your learner has gained the required skills, knowledge and understanding needed at a given point in time. It also provides your learners with an opportunity to demonstrate what progress they have made, and appreciate what they have achieved so far.
>
> This chapter will explore your role as an assessor, along with the concepts and principles which underpin it.
>
> This chapter will cover the following topics:
>
> - The role of assessment
> - Roles and responsibilities of an assessor
> - The assessment cycle
> - Concepts and principles of assessment

The role of assessment

Assessment can take place in any environment, for example a classroom, a training workshop, the workplace or an outside location. It is a measure of learning at a given point which demonstrates your learner's progress and achievement. The results of assessment can be used towards a learner gaining a certificate and/or a qualification, or to confirm their competent performance at work. It is therefore important that you carry out your assessor role correctly and in compliance with all the relevant requirements. Being an assessor can be very rewarding as you will be confirming your learner's progress and achievements. Think of it as a skilled profession with a responsibility for your learner's future.

You will need to know who and what you are going to assess, when and where it will take place, and how you will go about it. If you are currently assessing, you will probably know this already; if you are new to assessing, you will need to find this out. If you don't plan for and carry out any assessment with your learners, you will not know what, and how well, they have learnt. The type of employment contract you have and where you are based will have an influence on how often you see your learners. It will depend on whether, for example, you are full time, part time, freelance or self-employed, and if you are based in the same environment as your learner or not.

If you see your learners regularly, you can assess that learning is taking place each time you are with them. This is called *informal* assessment and could simply be by watching what your learner is doing and/or asking questions to check their knowledge and understanding. *Formal* assessment will count towards the achievement of something, whereas informal assessment is to check progress. However, assessment should not be in isolation from the teaching and learning process. For example, if you are assessing in the workplace, you (or someone else) might carry out a short training session if your learner hasn't quite met the requirements. Alternatively, you might be assessing an online programme where you never meet your learner, but they will be working through training materials beforehand.

There are some assessors who do not teach or train, but will just assess, make decisions and give feedback. This might be where competent staff are demonstrating their skills towards their job role, or are being assessed towards performance management or service standards. These assessors might be employed in the same organisation as their learners, be freelance, or might work for a college or training organisation and visit the learners in the workplace as required. You will find more information about assessing in different contexts in Chapter 2.

There is a difference between assessment *for* learning, and assessment *of* learning. Assessment *for* learning is usually a *formative* process and is often informal. It will ascertain the progress made so far in order to plan further learning and development. It's called formative assessment as it is ongoing throughout the learning process. Assessment *of* learning is usually *summative* and often formal, and confirms that learning and achievement have taken place. It's called summative assessment as it occurs at the end of an aspect of learning.

If your learners are working towards a qualification, there will be *formal summative* methods of assessment you will need to use such as an assignment, or a workplace observation. However, you can devise *informal formative* methods to use with your learners to check their progress at any time, such as role-plays or quizzes. Assessment should always focus on improving and reinforcing learning as well as measuring progress and achievements. It should help your learners realise how they are progressing and what they need to do to improve and/or develop further.

Example

Jamie has devised an informal formative quiz based on a popular television programme. He uses it to ask questions to his group of learners at the end of each theory session. Using it also introduces an element of fun to the subject. The quiz is to assess knowledge progress towards the Level 1 Motor Vehicle Studies qualification. Jamie then uses the formal summative activities provided by the awarding organisation to assess each learner's achievement at the appropriate time.

Assessment should be a regular and continual process; it might not always be formalised, but you might be informally watching what your learners are doing, asking them questions, and reviewing their progress whenever you are in contact with them. If you also teach or train, your learners will be demonstrating their skills, knowledge and understanding regularly, for example through tasks, discussions and activities. It's good practice to give your learners feedback when assessing them informally to help them realise what progress they are making. If they haven't reached a certain standard, you should still give feedback on what they have done well so far, and how they can improve and develop further. This will help retain their motivation. If you feel it is difficult to make an objective decision with the assessment activities used, you will need to discuss your concerns with other staff, or with a contact from the awarding organisation. You may need to redesign some activities to make them more specific and/or unambiguous. If all your learners are achieving everything with ease, perhaps you need to be more challenging with the tasks you set. You will find more information regarding making decisions and providing feedback in Chapter 4.

Assessment can help your learners by:

- acknowledging what progress has been made

- addressing issues where there are gaps in learning

- ascertaining areas for development

- confirming achievements

- diagnosing any areas of concern to enable support to be arranged

- encouraging discussions and questions

- ensuring they are on the right programme at the right level

- identifying what is yet to be learnt and achieved

- maintaining motivation

- seeing any inaccuracies, for example spelling errors in a written task or mistakes during a practical task.

If your subject or qualification is quality assured, internal and external quality assurers will sample your work to ensure your judgements and decisions are correct and fair. You will find more about quality assurance in Chapter 5. Some learners might have a mentor: someone who is supporting and encouraging them while they go through the learning and assessment process. They may also have other teachers or trainers who will assess them. However, do be aware of any sensitive or confidential issues relating to your learners which they may not wish you to pass on. Conversely, you may need to inform others of any particular learner requirements to ensure consistency of support.

You are therefore constantly making judgements and should be aware of the impact that your comments can have on your learner's confidence when you give feedback. Imagine how you feel when you receive feedback, perhaps elated because the comments are good, but demoralised if not. Comments which specifically focus on the activity or the work produced, rather than the individual as a person, will be more helpful and motivating. Assessment should not become a personal or *subjective* judgement, but should be *objective* and relate to the activity or criteria being assessed.

Think back to the last time you gave feedback to someone for something they did. Were you objective *by focusing on what was achieved, or were you* subjective *by becoming personal and deviating from what they had achieved? How do you think this made the person feel?*

The starting point for assessment

If you are going to assess accredited qualifications, the starting point should be the *programme handbook*, often known as a *qualification specification*. An accredited qualification is via an awarding organisation who will issue a certificate to a learner upon successful achievement. The qualification specification should state how your subject should be assessed and quality assured, and is usually available from the awarding organisation's website. It will give information and guidance in the form of an *assessment strategy*. This should state the experience, professional development and qualifications that assessors and internal quality assurers should have. It will also state how the subject should be assessed, and whether assessment activities are provided for you, or if you need to create your own. Alternatively, you might be assessing non-accredited qualifications, which are programmes of learning which do not lead to a formal qualification or a certificate issued by an awarding organisation. However, a company certificate of achievement might be issued as proof of success.

If you are going to assess learners in the workplace, for example their competence or performance, the starting point should be the company or service standards, or the job specifications. Looking at these will help you plan effective activities to assess skills, knowledge and understanding, based on what the learners know already. You will need to discuss them with your learner and their supervisor to ensure that you all interpret the requirements in the same way. Standards often change, therefore you would need to ensure that you are working with the latest version.

The reasons for assessment

The reasons for assessment can be separated into those of the learner, yourself as the assessor, your organisation, and the awarding organisation (if applicable) (see Table 1.1).

Assessment should not be confused with evaluation; assessment is of *learning*, evaluation is of the *programme* that the learner is taking, for example, a qualification. Assessment is specific towards an individual learner's progress and achievements, as well as identifying how they can develop and improve. Evaluation is a quality assurance monitoring tool. It includes obtaining feedback from your learners and others, such as employers, line managers and quality assurers, to help you improve the overall learner experience, as well as your own practice. You will find more information regarding evaluation in Chapter 6.

Table 1.1 Examples of the reasons for assessment

Learner	Assessor
• To clarify what is expected of them • To enable discussions with assessors • To evaluate their own progress • To have something to show for their achievements, for example a certificate • To help them plan and achieve their aim • To know how well they are progressing • To know what they have achieved • To know they are working at the correct standard or level • To know what they have to do to improve and progress further • To learn from their mistakes	• To adapt teaching, learning and assessment activities • To ascertain learners' progress and achievement so far • To assess in a consistent, fair and ethical manner • To carry out all aspects of the assessment cycle and keep records • To develop learners' self-assessment skills • To identify any learner needs or particular learning requirements • To empower learners to take control of their learning • To follow the requirements of the awarding organisation, programme or criteria being assessed • To improve learner motivation and self-esteem • To make decisions and give feedback • To prepare learners for further assessments • To maintain an audit trail of achievements • To prove they can assess effectively • To standardise judgements and practice with others
Organisation	**Awarding organisation**
• To achieve funding (if applicable) • To analyse enrolment, retention, success and achievement rates • To ensure adequate resources are available • To ensure consistency of assessors' practice and decisions • To give references for learners if requested • To identify gaps in learning • To incorporate assessment into an effective internal quality assurance system • To justify delivery of programmes • To monitor progression • To promote a learner-centred approach • To satisfy external requirements	• To accredit achievements • To ensure compliance with regulations and qualification requirements • To ensure staff follow the assessment strategy • To sample assessment and internal quality assurance (IQA) activities • To give guidance to assessors and internal quality assurers • To issue certificates • To formulate qualifications from recognised national occupational standards (NOS) • To provide reports regarding quality and compliance

If you are assessing learners who are working towards an accredited quali-fication, find out who the awarding organisation is for your particular subject and access their website. Locate the qualification specification and look at the assessment strategy to ensure you can meet the requirements. If you are going to assess non-accredited programmes of learning, obtain and familiarise yourself with the standards you will assess. If you are not currently assessing, have a look at some qualification specifications to familiarise yourself with their content.

Roles and responsibilities of an assessor

Your main role will be to plan and carry out assessments according to the qualification requirements, or those of any other criteria you will be assessing. You might also need to teach, train or coach your learners if required. This might take place off the job, for example in a college or training workshop, or on the job, for example if you are assessing an apprentice at work. You should therefore use appropriate assessment methods, make decisions and give feedback to your learners on an ongoing basis. You should communicate with others who have an interest in your learner's progress, such as their supervisor at work. At the end of this section is a checklist which you might find useful to ensure you are performing your role of an assessor correctly.

If you are already employed as an assessor, you should have a job description which outlines your roles and responsibilities. However, you might be freelance or work for an agency and not have anything specific to follow. Working towards a recognised assessment qualification, or ensuring you are meeting the national occupational standards (NOS) for assessors will help make sure you are doing what you should.

Your roles and responsibilities might include the following:

- attending meetings, exhibitions, award ceremonies and presentation events
- checking the authenticity of any witness testimonies
- coaching learners as required
- completing and maintaining safe and secure records
- countersigning other assessors' judgements (if they are not yet qualified and you are)
- following relevant policies and procedures
- giving constructive, supportive and developmental feedback to your learners regarding progress and achievement
- identifying and dealing with any barriers to fair assessment
- implementing internal and external quality assurance action points
- inducting new learners, i.e. introducing them to the organisation, the facilities and staff, and what will be assessed

- liaising with others involved in the assessment process

- making judgements based on the assessment requirements

- negotiating and agreeing assessment plans with learners

- making best use of different types and methods of assessment

- providing statistics to managers and others

- reflecting upon your practice and maintaining your professional development

- responding to any appeals made against your assessment decisions

- reviewing learner progress

- standardising practice with other assessors

- supporting learners with special assessment requirements and dealing with sensitive issues in a supportive manner

- teaching, training or coaching learners

- working towards relevant assessment qualifications or standards.

If you are unsure of any aspect of your assessor role, make sure you ask a colleague or your supervisor. You may be the only assessor for your particular subject within your organisation, therefore it is important that you liaise with others to ensure that you are interpreting the requirements correctly. If you are a member of a team of assessors, you will need to ensure that you all work together to give your learners equal and fair access to assessment opportunities. If there are several assessors for the same subject, there will be a co-ordinating or lead assessor who will manage the team and give support and advice regarding the assessment process. The team should meet regularly to standardise their practice so that everyone assesses in a consistent manner.

Your role will require you to use various assessment activities, which can take place in different environments depending upon what is being assessed and why.

Example

- **Classroom or training room** – *practical and theoretical tasks, tests, discussions, role-plays, projects, and presentations.*

- **Lecture theatre or hall** – *exams, multiple choice tests, and written questions.*

- **Library or home** – *assignments, online activities, research and reading.*

- **Outside environment** – *practical activities and projects.*

- **Workplace** – *observations, questions, and reviewing products and evidence produced by learners.*

- **Workshop** – *simulations and practical activities and tests.*

Wherever you are assessing, you will need to ensure that both you and your learners are suitably prepared, and that you follow the assessment requirements and relevant guidelines. If you haven't been told what these are, you will need to ask someone you work with.

Part of your role as an assessor will also be to inspire and motivate your learners. If you are enthusiastic and passionate about your subject, this will help to encourage, motivate and challenge your learners to progress further. Your learners may already be motivated for personal reasons and be enthusiastic and *want* to perform well. This is known as *intrinsic* motivation. They may be motivated by a *need* to learn, for example to gain a qualification, promotion or pay rise at work, known as *extrinsic* motivation. If you can recognise the difference between a learner's wants and needs, you can appreciate why they are motivated, and ensure that you make their experience meaningful and relevant. Whatever type of motivation your learners have will be transformed, for better or worse, by what happens during their assessment experience with you.

There will be certain records and documents that you will need to maintain. These will include assessment plans, feedback records, reviews of progress and overall tracking sheets. You will see examples of these as you work through the chapters in this book; however, they might differ from the ones you will be required to use. Records must be maintained to satisfy organisational and regulatory requirements. You should safely store confidential documents and audio/digital/video recordings that include images of learners, and you might need to seek a learner's permission prior to taking photos or visual recordings. You should always follow your organisation's data protection policy and the requirements of the Data Protection Act (1998).

Communication

You will not have a second chance to make a first impression, therefore it is important to portray yourself in a professional way when communicating with others. That's not only with what you say, but in the way you say it: your attitude, body language and dress. A warm and confident smile, positive attitude, self-assurance and the use of eye contact will all help when communicating, particularly if you are meeting someone for the first time. You might act differently depending upon the circumstances and who you are with, for example informally with colleagues, or formally with external quality assurers. Communication can be verbal, non-verbal or written (manual or electronic). Whichever method you use, communication is a means of passing on information from one person to another.

Skills of effective communication include the way you speak, listen and express yourself, with body language and written information. You need to be confident and organised with what you wish to convey; the way you do this will give an impression of yourself for better or worse. You may have to attend meetings or video conferences. Wherever you are with other people, they will make assumptions about you based on what they see and hear. You may have to write reports, memos or emails and the way you express yourself when writing is as important as when speaking.

When communicating verbally, your tone, pace and inflections are all important factors in getting your message across. If you speak too quickly or softly others may not hear everything you say, so always try to speak clearly. It is useful to consider what reactions you want to achieve from the information you are communicating, and if others react differently, you will need to amend your methods. You might be communicating via the telephone, therefore unable to see any reactions to what you say, which could lead to a misunderstanding. Always ask questions to check that the person you are communicating with has understood what you have said. Non-verbal communication includes your body language and posture, for example gestures and the way you stand or sit. Be conscious of your mannerisms, such as folded arms or hands in pockets, or the gestures you make, and use eye contact with the person you are communicating with. The things you don't say are just as important as what you do say.

Written communication, for example in the form of feedback for assessed work, is also an expression of you as a person. The way you convey your words and phrases, and your intention, may not be how it is read or understood by the other person. There are always different ways of interpreting the same event. If you are working with learners via an online programme, you may never see them, but will probably build up a visual image; they may therefore be doing the same of you. Information can be easily misinterpreted; the sender has to be sure the receiver will interpret any communication in the way that it was intended. You need to get your message across effectively, otherwise what you are conveying may not necessarily reflect your own thoughts and may cause a breakdown in communication. Any written text cannot be taken back, so there is less room for errors or mistakes and you need to be clear about the exact meaning you wish to convey. Your writing should be checked for spelling, grammar and punctuation. Don't rely on a computer to check these, as it will not always realise the context in which you are writing. This is particularly the case when writing feedback to learners; if you make a spelling mistake, they will think the word is correct, as you are deemed to be the more knowledgeable person.

You might give feedback to your learners via the internet, for example by using email or a web-based system. If you use this type of medium for communication and/or assessment purposes, try not to get into the habit of abbreviating words or cutting out vowels. It is important to express yourself in a professional way, otherwise misunderstanding and confusion may arise. Just imagine you are talking to the other person, and type your message appropriately and professionally.

If your organisation takes on new assessors, you might be asked to mentor and support them. If they are unqualified and you are already a qualified assessor, you might also be asked to countersign their decisions to ensure they are valid and fair. New staff should be given an induction to the assessment policy and procedures, all relevant paperwork, systems and organisational requirements. If an assessor is leaving, there should be a system of succession planning, to allow time for an appropriate handover, and any relevant training to take place. Usually, the awarding organisation will need to be informed of any staff changes, to ensure that new staff are suitably qualified and experienced.

You could have learners who have excelled in some way, and your organisation or awarding organisation might have an award or medal for which they could be nominated. Your own organisation or department might hold a celebration event to present certificates to successful learners. This is also a way of obtaining positive publicity for your organisation, valuing and celebrating the success of your learners.

Communicating with others

You will need to communicate with other people if they are involved in the assessment process of your learners. These people might be internal to your organisation (i.e. administrative staff) or external (i.e. employers). You should remain professional at all times as you are representing your organisation. People might not always remember your name, however, and you may be known as 'that person from XYZ organisation'. You therefore need to create a good and lasting impression of yourself and your organisation. In some organisations, you may be required to wear a name badge, carry identification, and sign in and out for security reasons.

You will need to know what information can be available to help support the assessment process for your learners and the others who are involved. For example, information such as the standards or units to be assessed, progress and achievement records, assessment plans and feedback documentation, and resources such as text books, internet websites and journals that will prove useful. Workplace supervisors, mentors and witnesses will need details of your learner's progress and achievements. Learning support staff will need relevant information regarding your learner to provide any necessary help and guidance. Communicating regularly will ensure everyone who is involved with your learner knows of their progress and achievement, and what else might be required.

You might need to liaise with support staff, perhaps to arrange help with preparing and copying assessment materials and resources, or by making modifications or adaptations to equipment and materials. You might also need to get in touch with others who have an interest in your learners, such as parents, probation officers or social workers. If this is the case, follow procedures for confidentiality and data protection, and keep notes of all discussions in case you need to refer to them again.

If you have learners who are attending a programme in conjunction with a school, college or other organisation, you may need to liaise with their staff in order to give reports of progress and attendance. You may need to communicate with employers, managers or supervisors whose staff you are assessing in the workplace. If this is the case, make sure you are aware of any protocols involved, and follow your organisation's procedures for dealing with external clients.

You might teach a particular subject, but not assess it; for example, your learners may take an exam which is marked by awarding organisation personnel, or a test which is marked by a colleague. You might have to plan for examinations to take place, in which case you will need to ensure the administrative staff are aware of what will happen and when, as invigilators may be needed, secure storage will be required for papers, and specific rooms timetabled accordingly.

If you are not the only assessor for your subject, you will need to standardise your practice with other assessors. If you are assessing an academic qualification, you might use the term *double marking* or *second marking* rather than standardisation. This enables different assessors to mark one another's assessed work, to ensure the correct grade has been given. This could take place blindly, i.e. you don't get to see the original grade. Having a marking scheme or expected answers will help you reach a fair decision. If standardisation is not carried out, assessment activities and decisions might not be fair to all learners. You will find more information regarding standardising practice in Chapter 5.

Examples of other people you may need to communicate with include:

- administration staff – to register and certificate learners with an awarding organisation

- awarding organisation personnel – to ensure compliance with their regulations

- co-tutors – to provide information on progress

- finance staff – to help with funding, grants and loans

- internal quality assurers – to ensure the assessment process is fair

- learning support staff – to provide support to learners as necessary

- managers – to ensure organisational procedures are followed

- other teachers, trainers and assessors – to communicate information regarding learner progress and achievement

- safeguarding officers – to help ensure the well-being of learners

- support workers – to provide help and support when needed

- workplace supervisors and employers – to provide information regarding progress and achievements

- work placement co-ordinators – to arrange and monitor suitable work experience placements.

Activity

Find out who you need to communicate with, either internally or externally, regarding the subjects you are assessing. How can you contact them and why would you? Make a note of telephone numbers, addresses, websites, email addresses, etc. which could come in useful.

Knowing who you need to communicate with, how you should proceed, and what is involved in the communication process should make your role as an assessor more rewarding and professional.

You might find the following checklist useful to ensure you are performing your role of an assessor correctly. If any aspects don't make sense yet, they should become clearer as you work through the chapters of this book.

Assessor checklist

☐ Do I need to achieve an assessor qualification? If so, do I know how to apply and who will support me until I am qualified?

☐ Do I need to participate in any continuing professional development (CPD)? If so, what and when?

☐ Should I be demonstrating my knowledge and skills towards a set of national occupational standards (NOS)? If so, do I know where to locate these?

☐ Is there an assessment strategy which states what qualifications and experience I must have to assess my learners? If so, do I meet the requirements or is there anything I need to do?

☐ Do I have a copy of the qualification specification, standards or criteria for the subject I will be assessing? If not, do I know how to obtain and use it effectively?

☐ Do I understand the awarding organisation's requirements for the qualification I will assess? If not, who can I ask?

☐ What meetings do I need to attend, and when?

☐ Do I have the opportunity to standardise my practice with other assessors? If so, when is the next event?

☐ When will my internal quality assurer observe my practice? Do I know who they are and how I can get in touch with them?

☐ Have all my learners been registered with the awarding organisation (if applicable)?

☐ What is the induction procedure I must go through with a new learner?

☐ Do I know the procedure for claiming certificates or issuing records of achievement/ attendance? If not, is there anything I need to do or anyone I need to liaise with?

☐ Am I familiar with all relevant policies and procedures? If not, how do I find out about them?

☐ Do I need to carry out any initial or diagnostic assessments with my learners? If so, what do I need to do?

☐ Can I complete individual assessment/action plans with each learner, with suitable dates, times and assessment methods, taking into account any particular individual needs? Is there a facility to give each learner a copy, either manual or electronic?

☐ Do I need to liaise with anyone else, for example workplace supervisors? If so, how do I go about this?

☐ Can I differentiate the assessment activities if necessary? Do I need to inform anyone, such as the awarding organisation?

☐ How can I utilise new and emerging technologies for assessment purposes?

☐ Do I need to produce questions or assignments with expected responses? Should I standardise these with anyone else?

☐ What specific assessment records will I need to complete and why?

☐ Do I know the requirements for keeping records? If not, what are they?

☐ Do I feel confident at making assessment decisions which are fair and ethical, and can I give feedback in a constructive way?

☐ How can I ensure the assessed work meets standards of validity, authenticity, currency, sufficiency and reliability (VACSR)?

☐ What do I do if a learner appeals against my decision or makes a complaint against me?

Extension Activity

What do you consider your roles and responsibilities are as an assessor? Make a list and place them in order of importance. You might consider some roles to be responsibilities as they can be interpreted differently depending upon what you do and where you work.

The assessment cycle

The assessment cycle is a systematic process which should be followed to give your learner a positive experience. Depending upon the subject you are assessing and whether it is academic (theory or knowledge based) or vocational (practical or performance based), you will usually follow the assessment cycle (see Figure 1.1).

The cycle will continue until all aspects of the programme or qualification have hopefully been achieved by your learner, or perhaps not if they decide to leave.

Throughout the cycle, standardisation of assessment practice between assessors should take place; this will help ensure the consistency and fairness of decisions, and that all assessors interpret the requirements in the same way. Internal quality assurance might also take place throughout as part of the quality assurance process.

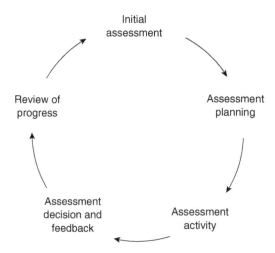

Figure 1.1 Assessment cycle

• **Initial assessment** – ascertaining if your learner has any previous knowledge and/ or experience of the subject or area to be assessed. This information can be obtained through application forms, interviews and discussions. The results of initial assessment activities will give you information regarding your learners: for example, any specific assessment requirements they may have or any further training and support they may need. This process might not always be carried out by you, but the information obtained must be passed on to you. Initial assessment is known as assessment *for* learning, as it helps prepare learners *for* assessment and identifies their potential.

- **Assessment planning** – agreeing suitable types and methods of assessment with learners, setting appropriate target dates, involving others as necessary (such as colleagues or supervisors).

- **Assessment activity** – using relevant methods, approaches and activities, for example observation, questioning, assignments, or gathering appropriate evidence of competence. Assessment can be formative (usually ongoing and informal to check progress, e.g. a discussion) and/or summative (usually at the end and formal, e.g. a test). Summative assessment is often known as assessment *of* learning as it counts towards the achievement *of* something.

- **Assessment decision and feedback** – making a judgement of success or otherwise, or allocating a grade and advising how to achieve a higher grade in future. Providing constructive feedback and agreeing any further action that may be necessary.

- **Review of progress** – reviewing progress and achievement, discussing any other issues that may be relevant to the learning and assessment process.

Records should be maintained throughout all aspects of the assessment cycle, and quality assurance activities should take place on an ongoing basis. The cycle will then begin again with an initial assessment regarding the next area to be assessed. You will find more information regarding record keeping in Chapter 4.

As an internal quality assurer only samples various activities, there is the possibility some aspects might be missed. Imagine quality assurance taking place in a bakery. Every product from every batch would not be sampled, for example, by taking a bite of each one. This way, 100 per cent sampling would be taking place and there would be nothing left to sell. One item from each batch might therefore be sampled. There are risks involved and these should be considered when planning the sampling strategy. For example, if an assessor is new to the role, their work should be sampled more.

Policies and procedures

Throughout the cycle, you will need to take into account relevant policies and procedures. You should be made aware of these when you commence your role, if not, make sure you find out where you can access them. They could include:

- access and fair assessment
- appeals
- authenticity
- complaints
- confidentiality of information

- copyright and data protection

- equality and diversity

- health, safety and welfare

- plagiarism

- quality assurance

- safeguarding and Prevent Duty.

If you are a work-based trainer and/or assessor, you may have to design your training and assessment activities around the company's policies and procedures (sometimes called *method statements* or *work instructions*). These will usually have the relevant legislation such as aspects of health and safety, and equality and diversity built into them.

Legislation, regulatory requirements and codes of practice

Legislation relates to laws passed by Parliament, regulatory requirements are usually specific to certain industries, and codes of practice vary depending upon the organisation within which you will work. It is important for you to keep up to date with all of this to ensure that you are remaining current with your skills, knowledge and understanding, and with any changes or updates that may have taken place.

Example

Abdul is a part-time assessor for the Level 3 Health and Social Care qualification. He visits his learners in different organisations on a regular basis. He soon realised that there is a lot of legislation, regulatory requirements and codes of practice, that both his learners and he must follow. Once a week, he takes the time to search the internet for appropriate websites to see if anything has changed. After some recent developments, he gave each of his learners a handout summarising these. He also makes sure he is up to date with the policies and procedures of the organisation he works for by checking them on the company intranet.

Legislation
Legislation will differ depending upon the context and environment within which you will assess. You need to be aware of the requirements of external bodies and regulators such as Ofsted (in England) who inspect provision, along with awarding organisations who will quality assure their qualifications, and funding agencies who will need data and statistics.

The following information was current at the time of writing; however, you are advised to check for any changes or updates, and whether or not they are applicable outside England. You will find more information regarding safeguarding, health and safety, and equality and diversity in Chapter 2.

Children Act (2004) will be applicable to you if you work with 14–19 year olds, vulnerable adults or learners with special needs.

Counter-Terrorism and Security Act (2015) will apply if you work with learners who are at risk of becoming radicalised. The Prevent Duty is part of this Act.

Copyright Designs and Patents Act (1988) relates to the copying, adapting and distributing of materials, which includes computer programs and materials found via the internet. Organisations may have a licence to enable the photocopying of small amounts from books or journals. All copies should have the source acknowledged.

Data Protection Act (1998) made provision for the regulation of the processing of information relating to individuals, including the obtaining, holding, use or disclosure of such information. It was amended in 2003 to include electronic data.

The Equality Act (2010) replaced all previous anti-discrimination legislation and consolidated it into one Act (for England, Scotland and Wales). It provides rights for people not to be directly discriminated against or harassed because they have an association with a disabled person or because they are wrongly perceived as disabled.

Freedom of Information Act (2000) gives learners the opportunity to request to see the information public bodies hold about them.

Health and Safety at Work etc. Act (1974) imposes obligations on all staff within an organisation commensurate with their role and responsibility. Risk assessments should be carried out where necessary. In the event of an accident, particularly one resulting in death or serious injury, an investigation by the Health and Safety Executive may result in the prosecution of individuals found to be negligent as well as the organisation.

Protection of Children Act (POCA) (1999) was designed to protect children. It gives responsibility to local authorities to make enquiries when anyone contacts them with concerns about child abuse.

Rehabilitation of Offenders Act (1974) will be applicable if you work with ex-offenders.

Safeguarding Vulnerable Groups Act (2006) introduced a vetting and barring scheme to make decisions about who should be barred from working with children and vulnerable adults. Assessors may need to apply to the Disclosure and Barring Service (DBS) to have a criminal record check. The purpose of the DBS is to help employers prevent unsuitable people from working with children and vulnerable adults.

Welsh Language Act (1993) put the Welsh language on an equal footing with the English language in Wales, with regard to the public sector.

Regulatory requirements
Regulations are often called *rules* and they specify mandatory requirements that must be met. Public bodies, corporations, agencies and organisations create regulatory requirements which must be followed if they are applicable to your job role. In education, for example, one of the regulators is Ofqual, which regulates qualifications, examinations and assessments in England, and vocational qualifications in Northern Ireland. Ofqual

gives formal recognition to awarding organisations and bodies that deliver and award qualifications. There will also be specific regulations which relate to your specialist subject and you will need to find out what these are. Examples include the following.

Control of Substances Hazardous to Health (COSHH) Regulations (2002) applies if you work with hazardous materials.

Food Hygiene Regulations (2006) applies to aspects of farming, manufacturing, distributing and retailing food.

Health and Safety (Display screen equipment) Regulations (1992) applies to using display screen equipment, for example, computers.

Manual Handling Operation Regulations (1992) relates to hazards of manual handling and risks of injury.

Privacy and Electronic Communications (EC Directive) Regulations 2003 applies to all electronic communications such as email and mobile phone messages.

Reporting of Injuries, Diseases and Dangerous Occurrences (RIDDOR) Regulations (1995) requires specified workplace incidents to be reported.

Regulatory Reform (Fire Safety) Order (2005) places the responsibility on individuals within an organisation to carry out risk assessments to identify, manage and reduce the risk of fire.

Codes of practice

Codes of practice are usually produced by organisations, associations and professional bodies. They can be mandatory or voluntary and you will need to find out which are applicable to your job role. If you belong to any professional associations, they will usually have a code of practice for you to follow; for example, the Society for Education and Training (SET) has a Code of Professional Practice (2008). This was inherited from the (no longer operational) Institute for Learning (IfL). There are other professional associations such as the Chartered Institute for Educational Assessors (CIEA), the Institute for Leadership and Management (ILM), and the Institute of Training and Occupational Learning (ITOL), which you could join.

In addition, your organisation should have documented codes of practice which you will need to follow, such as:

- acceptable use of information and communication technology (ICT)

- code of conduct

- confidentiality of information

- conflict of interest

- disciplinary

- duty of care to learners, including personal development, behaviour and welfare

- duty to prevent radicalisation

- environmental awareness
- lone working
- misconduct
- sustainability.

Activity

Think about the legislation, regulatory requirements and codes of practice which will relate to your role as an assessor for your particular subject. Which are the most important and why? How will they impact upon the assessment process?

Professional boundaries

Boundaries are about knowing where your role as an assessor stops. You should be able to work within the limits of that role, but know that it's okay to ask for help. There are two aspects to boundaries: those between your assessing role and other professional roles, and other aspects you are *bound by* which might hinder or challenge your role.

- Professional boundaries are those within which you need to work and it's important not to overstep these, for example by becoming too personal or friendly with your learners. Don't try to take on too much, or carry out something which is part of someone else's role.

- Other boundaries include the things you are bound by, for example policies and procedures, the amount of administrative work you are expected to complete, or a lack of funding or resources. These boundaries can often be interpreted as the negative aspects of your roles and responsibilities.

You might have other professional roles besides assessing; for example, you might interview learners and have to decide whether they can attend a programme or not. If you make a decision not to accept a learner onto a programme, you will need to justify your reasons. Never feel you are on your own; find out who can give help and advice when you need it. If you are a new assessor, you might have been allocated a *mentor* and/or someone to check and countersign your assessment decisions. They should support you as necessary and you will find it helpful to keep in touch with them and ask for advice when needed.

When you are with learners, you need to remain in control, be fair and ethical with your practice, and not demonstrate any favouritism towards particular learners: for example, by giving one more support than another. You might feel it sensible to make a telephone call to a learner who has been absent, but making regular calls would be inappropriate. Giving your personal telephone number to learners could be seen as encouraging informal contact, and you may get calls or texts which are not suitable or relevant. You might not want to take your break with your learners or join their social networking sites as you could be seen as more of a friend than an assessor. It is unprofessional to use bad language or to let your personal problems affect your work.

What do you consider the boundaries of your role to be? This might include teaching and training as well as assessment. You could look back at your list of roles and responsibilities to prompt you. If you are not currently assessing, think about this hypothetically.

Concepts and principles of assessment

Concepts of assessment relate to *ideas*, whereas principles are how the ideas are put into practice. For the purpose of this section, they have been separated for clarity; however, some concepts could also be classed as principles, depending upon your interpretation.

Concepts

Think of concepts as the aspects involved throughout the assessment process. They include the following (which are explained in detail below):

- accountability
- achievement
- assessment strategies
- benchmarking
- evaluation
- internally or externally devised assessment methods (formal and informal)
- progression
- transparency
- types of assessment, e.g. initial (at the beginning), formative (ongoing) or summative (at the end).

Accountability – you need to be accountable to your learners and your organisation to ensure that you are carrying out your role as an assessor correctly. Your learners should know why they are being assessed and what they have to do to meet the assessment criteria. You should not be assessing your learners on a summative basis unless they are ready. However, formative assessments can be used at any time to check progress. You will also be accountable to the awarding organisation if you assess their accredited qualifications. You might be accountable to employers if you are assessing their staff in the workplace.

Achievement – you may be required to analyse achievement data and compare this to national or organisational targets. The funding your organisation receives might also be related to your learners' achievements. It's always a useful evaluation method to keep a record of how many learners you start with, how many successfully achieve, their progression routes, and in what timescales.

Assessment strategy – following the assessment strategy for your subject will ensure you are carrying out your role correctly and holding or working towards the required assessor qualifications or standards if applicable.

Benchmarking – this involves comparing what is the accepted standard for a particular subject area against the current position of your own learners' performance. Using benchmarking data can help inform target setting for individuals or groups. If learners don't achieve the benchmark, an evaluation will need to take place and improvements will need to be implemented. Benchmarking can also be used to compare organisations that provide a similar service, or used within the same organisation to compare performance in different locations.

Evaluation of the assessment process – an evaluation should always take place to inform current and future practice. All aspects of the assessment cycle should be evaluated on an ongoing basis and feedback obtained from everyone involved.

Internally devised assessments – these might be produced by you or other staff at your organisation, such as assignments, projects or questions which will also be marked internally. These should always be appropriate, relevant, and at the right level for your learners. *Externally devised assessments* are usually produced by an awarding organisation, for example an examination. *Formal* assessments usually count towards achievement of a qualification, whereas *informal* assessments are used to monitor ongoing progress and development.

Progression – it is important to take progression into account when assessing learners, i.e. what they are going to do next. It could be another unit of the current qualification, or a different aspect of a job description, either at your organisation, in the workplace or elsewhere. Progression opportunities should always be discussed with your learners to ensure they are on the right route and that they are capable of achieving.

Transparency – to assist transparency, you need to ensure that everyone who is involved in the assessment process clearly understands what is expected and can see there is nothing untoward taking place. That includes your own interpretation and understanding of the assessment requirements as well as each learner's understanding. You should be honest with your learners and not let them feel they have achieved more than they have. Transparency is also about having nothing to hide and being open to scrutiny, i.e. keeping auditable records which must be maintained throughout the assessment process.

Types of assessment – these include initial, formative and summative. Initial assessment is carried out prior to or at the beginning of a programme to identify your learner's starting point, potential and level. Formative assessment is ongoing, and summative assessment is at the end of something, such as a task, a unit, a module or a qualification. You will find more information about types of assessment in Chapter 2.

Activity

Look at the bulleted list of concepts on page 20. Describe how each will impact upon your role as an assessor. Add any other aspects you feel are relevant but which have not yet been covered. You may need to research some aspects further or speak to relevant staff at your organisation.

Principles

Think of principles as *how* the concepts are put into practice.

One important principle is known by the acronym VACSR. You will need to ensure all assessed work is:

- **V**alid – the work is relevant to what is being assessed, and is at the right level.
- **A**uthentic – the work has been produced solely by the learner.
- **C**urrent – the work is still relevant at the time of assessment.
- **S**ufficient – the work covers all the requirements at the time.
- **R**eliable – the work is consistent over time.

If the above are not ensured, you might make an incorrect judgement and a learner might appeal against your decision. Conversely, you might not notice a learner has plagiarised someone else's work or done something incorrectly.

Example

Meena wanted to follow the VACSR principle when observing her learner, Jo, towards an aspect of the Level 2 Hairdressing qualification. She observed Jo with her client and made sure she was doing what was required, at the right level (V). As it was only Jo involved with the client, she knew it was authentic (A), and it was current as the activity was live (C). When Jo had finished her client's hairstyle, Meena asked a few questions to confirm her knowledge (S). This particular hairstyle was one Jo had demonstrated before, therefore her work was reliable and consistent (R).

Other principles of assessment can include:

- **Communication** – taking place regularly with learners, other assessors, internal quality assurers, employers and others who are involved.
- **Continuing professional development (CPD)** – maintaining the currency of skills, knowledge and understanding to ensure your assessment practice and subject knowledge are up to date.
- **Equality and diversity** – ensuring all assessment activities embrace equality, inclusivity and diversity, and represent all aspects of society.
- **Ethics** – ensuring the assessment process is honest and moral, and takes into account confidentiality and integrity.
- **Fairness** – ensuring assessment activities are fit for purpose, and planning, decisions and feedback justifiable. All learners should have an equal chance of an accurate assessment decision.

- **Health and safety** – ensuring these are taken into account throughout the full assessment process, carrying out risk assessments as necessary.

- **Motivation** – encouraging and supporting your learners to reach their maximum potential at an appropriate level.

- **Quality assurance** – ensuring assessment activities and decisions meet the required standards.

- **Record keeping** – ensuring accurate records are maintained throughout the assessment process.

- **Responsibility** – making objective decisions, following all organisational guidelines, keeping records and producing reports as required.

- **SMART** – ensuring all assessment activities are **S**pecific, **M**easurable, **A**chievable, **R**elevant and **T**imebound.

- **Standardisation** – ensuring the assessment requirements are interpreted accurately and that all assessors are making comparable and consistent decisions.

Extension Activity

Look at the above lists of principles of assessment. Describe how each will impact upon your role as an assessor. Add any other aspects you feel are relevant but which have not been covered in this chapter. You may need to research some areas further or speak to relevant staff at your organisation. Using your response to the last activity regarding concepts, make one full list of the key concepts and principles of assessment which are most relevant to you and your job role.

Summary

Following the key concepts and principles of assessment will ensure you are performing your role as an assessor according to all the relevant regulations and requirements. It will also help you support your learners towards achieving their chosen goal.

You might like to carry out further research by accessing the books and websites listed at the end of this chapter.

This chapter has covered the following topics:

- The role of assessment

- Roles and responsibilities of an assessor

- The assessment cycle

- Concepts and principles of assessment

References and further information

Bonnerjea, L. (2009) *Safeguarding Adults: Report on the Consultation on the Review of 'No Secrets'*. London: Department of Health.

Department for Education and Skills (DfES) (2006) *Safeguarding Children and Safer Recruitment in Education*. London: DfES.

Ecclestone, K. (2005) *Understanding Assessment and Qualifications in Post-Compulsory Education and Training* (2nd edn). Ashford: NIACE.

Gravells, A. (2014) *Achieving your Assessment and Quality Assurance Units (TAQA)*. London: Learning Matters/SAGE.

Gravells, A. (2014) *The Award in Education and Training* (revised edn). London: Learning Matters/SAGE.

Gravells, A. and Simpson, S. (2014) *The Certificate in Education and Training*. London: Learning Matters/SAGE.

Gravells, A. and Simpson, S. (2012) *Equality and Diversity in the Lifelong Learning Sector* (2nd edn). Exeter: Learning Matters.

Ollin, R. and Tucker, J. (2012) *The Vocational Assessor Handbook* (5th edn). London: Kogan Page.

Read, H. (2011) *The Best Assessor's Guide*. Bideford: Read On Publications.

Tummons, J. (2011) *Assessing Learning in the Lifelong Learning Sector* (3rd edn). Exeter: Learning Matters.

Wilson, L. (2012) *Practical Teaching: A Guide to Assessment and Quality Assurance*. Andover: Cengage Learning.

Websites

Chartered Institute for Educational Assessors – **www.ciea.org.uk**

Counter-Terrorism and Security Act (2015) – **www.legislation.gov.uk/ukpga/2015/6/contents/enacted**

COSHH – **www.hse.gov.uk/coshh**

Data Protection Act – **www.legislation.gov.uk/ukpga/1998/29/contents**

Disability and the Equality Act – **http://tinyurl.com/2vzd5j**

Disclosure and Barring Service – **www.gov.uk/government/organisations/disclosure-and-barring-service/about**

Equality and Human Rights Commission – **www.equalityhumanrights.com**

Freedom of Information Act – **www.legislation.gov.uk/ukpga/2000/36/contents**

Health and Safety Executive – **www.hse.gov.uk**

Health and Safety resources – **www.hse.gov.uk/services/education/information.htm**

National occupational standards for learning and development (including assessors) – **http://tinyurl.com/oplss5u**

Office safety and risk assessments – **www.officesafety.co.uk**

Ofqual – **www.ofqual.gov.uk**

Prevent Duty and Safeguarding resources – **www.preventforfeandtraining.org.uk**

2 PLANNING FOR ASSESSMENT

Introduction

Planning is an important aspect of the assessment process. What is going to be assessed and when should be agreed with everyone who has an involvement with your learners. This might include supervisors in the work environment, or other assessors in a college or a training organisation. The planning process should identify what your learners already know and can do, and what they need to know and do. You will need to consider both short-term and long-term assessment activities which will complement the topics being assessed.

This chapter will explore how you can plan to assess your learners in different contexts, and how you can give relevant support as required.

This chapter will cover the following topics:

- Assessing occupational competence in the work environment
- Assessing vocational skills, knowledge and understanding
- Types of assessment
- Supporting learners

Assessing occupational competence in the work environment

If you are assessing learners, employees or apprentices in the work environment, you will need to confirm their competence towards a skill, a qualification, relevant standards, or their job role.

Examples of assessment in the work environment include:

- an employee demonstrating they can meet the required service standards or national occupations standards

- a member of staff being assessed towards a qualification

- an apprentice demonstrating their skills and knowledge

- an employee demonstrating their competence at meeting aspects of their job description or job role

- a member of staff demonstrating skills and knowledge for performance management reasons

- a member of the armed, emergency and uniformed services demonstrating their skills and ability

- a voluntary worker in a non-profit organisation demonstrating their competence in the hope of obtaining permanent employment.

Some organisations use the term *validate* when confirming an employee's competence; for example, if they are aiming to achieve a certain standard to gain a business contract, or to confirm their staff are performing their job role correctly. For the purpose of this chapter, the term *learner* will be used for anyone who is being assessed or validated in the work environment. Planning what to assess and when is a crucial phase of the assessment process. However, before you commence, you need to be fully conversant with what you are going to assess, where this will be, and any particular requirements and regulations for your particular subject. Assessment activities should be valid, i.e. relevant and at the right level for the learner. They should also be reliable, i.e. if the same assessment activity was used with other learners, a similar and consistent result would be obtained.

If you are assessing towards a qualification which is accredited through an awarding organisation, a certificate can be claimed upon successful completion. The awarding organisation will monitor the delivery, assessment and quality assurance of the qualification to ensure all their requirements are being met. If you have not already done so, you will need to obtain a copy of the qualification specification which will contain all the details regarding the assessment requirements.

Vocational qualifications are an excellent way for competent learners to demonstrate their skills, knowledge and understanding in their work environment and gain an accredited certificate. However, if there are aspects of the qualification with which they are not familiar, training will need to take place. An initial assessment would greatly help identify what may need to be learnt first, before any formal assessment takes place. If you are not familiar with how to teach or train, there are relevant qualifications you can take.

If you are assessing an employee's competence towards their job role or a new skill they are putting into practice, this is known as *non-accredited*, as a certificate will not be issued by an awarding organisation. However, a *record of achievement* might be given to the employee once they have proved their competence. This could be issued by their employer, or the organisation you are assessing on behalf of.

If you visit learners in their place of work, it is best to plan ahead to enable assessment of relevant activities at appropriate times. If you have several learners in the same or different locations, planning ahead will enable you to assess learners who are in close proximity. This will help to ease the time and cost spent travelling. Out of courtesy, notify your learner's supervisor or manager in advance, in case there is any reason they cannot accommodate you on a particular day. You will also need to check travel, transport and/or parking arrangements.

Activity

When you are planning to assess in the work environment, can you use public transport, or is there a company vehicle you can use? If you use your own vehicle, find out if you can reclaim any expenses. Are there any protocols you need to follow when visiting other organisations? If you are not sure, find out. You may need to confirm dates and times, carry appropriate photo identification or take personal protective equipment (PPE) with you.

If your learner works shifts or during the weekend, you will need to visit when they are working, as it isn't fair to ask them to change their work patterns just to suit you. If for any reason an assessment is cancelled, make sure a revised date is scheduled as soon as possible, and inform all concerned. Always confirm your visit one or two days beforehand just in case there is any reason the assessment cannot go ahead.

If you are assessing a qualification, the methods might be stated for you by the awarding organisation. If not, you will need to decide on what is most appropriate. Try to use a mixture of at least two or three different assessment activities to keep the process interesting, for example: observation, oral questions and looking at work produced by your learner. This way, you are ensuring you are assessing not only learner performance but knowledge and understanding too.

Assessment should be a two-way process between you and your learner; you need to plan what you are going to do, and they need to know what is expected of them and when. It could be that you will assess units or aspects in a different order from that stated in the qualification requirements. For example, instead of assessing Unit 1 before Unit 2, you might decide with your learner that Unit 2 could be assessed first, as they are already performing the requirements at work which are included in that unit. However, they might also naturally cover aspects of other units, which should not be discounted when you assess your learner, just because they weren't planned for.

The way you assess your learners will depend upon the following:

- assessment strategy from the awarding organisation (if applicable)
- dates, times and duration of assessment activities
- location and environment
- qualification/employment level
- types and methods of assessment
- organisational budget
- requirements for making decisions and giving feedback
- resources and materials available

- special assessment requirements or particular learner needs

- staff availability and expertise

- subject or topic being assessed.

The planning process should involve a discussion between you and your learner, with the chance to set realistic dates and targets. However, it could be that when you do assess your learner, they are not quite as ready as anticipated.

Example

Megan is assessing the Level 2 Floristry qualification. She visits each learner once a month in their place of work to observe their competence, and asks questions to check their knowledge. While carrying out an assessment with Ben, she realises he is not quite competent in the area she had planned to assess. Megan demonstrates how to perform one of the tasks expected and then Ben attempts it on his own. Megan asks Ben to practise this over the next few days and arranges to return the following month to carry out a formal assessment.

In this example, Megan has carried out an impromptu training session with Ben by demonstrating the task. She then encouraged him to do it himself while she was still present, and then on his own afterwards. Megan could assess other aspects of the qualification while she is there if Ben feels confident. In this way, the visit can still lead to an achievement. You will need to be patient with your learners as it takes time for them to consolidate learning and put theory into practice. At times you might just be assessing progress rather than achievement. However, don't let this demoralise your learner; try and keep them motivated to work towards achieving something.

If you do carry out training sessions and demonstrate something in front of learners, always check if they are left-handed or right-handed, as this could change the way they view things. Also, when they look at you, your right hand will be on their left. If you are demonstrating on a one-to-one basis, try to stand or sit next to your learner rather than facing them.

Assessment methods in the work environment

If you are assessing in the work environment, the most commonly used methods include:

- observations

- examining work products and evidence

- asking questions – written or oral

- holding discussions with your learner, often known as professional discussions

- obtaining witness testimonies; for example, from a learner's supervisor

- reading your learner's written statements of how they perform certain tasks, and confirming these with their supervisor

- recognising your learner's prior learning (RPL).

Some of these can also be used for assessing skills, knowledge and understanding (if relevant) in areas other than the work environment.

Observations

Observations of your learners enable you to see them performing skills in their normal working or training environment. However, observations should be backed up with questions to ensure your learner also has the knowledge and understanding to perform the skill. When observing, let your learner make a mistake (if it is safe) rather than interrupt them. You can then discuss this later to see if they realised what they had done. If you observe groups of learners, you would need to confirm what each individual learner has achieved. When observing, try to remain out of the way, but still in a position to see and hear what is going on. It's difficult to remain inconspicuous, and you might even find you get in the way of others if you are assessing in the workplace. When documenting the outcomes of an observation, your record will need to be detailed, stating what your learner has achieved and how they did it. If it's towards a qualification or set of standards, you should be specific about what has and hasn't been met. You could add the reference numbers to your document to denote which aspects have been achieved. Some organisations accept a video or digital recording of the observed activities, or allow the use of remote observations via the internet if you can't be there in person. You would need to find out if this is acceptable and, if so, under what conditions. This could include obtaining permissions from others who might appear in the recording.

Examining work products and evidence

Work products and evidence produced by your learners will be based around the work they have carried out: for example, letters, emails and reports that they have produced in an office (as long as they remain confidential). You would then decide if all the evidence successfully covered the criteria being assessed. Portfolios are often used by learners, whether manual and/or electronic, to store their evidence. These might also contain witness testimonies written by their supervisor in support of their work. Product evidence could include actual items the learner has constructed, such as an item that has been welded together in a factory. This would not fit in a portfolio, but the learner could state where the item is located and include photos or a recording of them making the product. You would need to see the real product to make a decision, and be satisfied your learner had completed the work themselves. It would be useful to get them to sign an authenticity statement to prove the work is theirs.

Asking questions – written or oral

Questions (written or oral) are a great way to assess knowledge and understanding and validate learning. Be careful if you are using the same questions for different learners, as they might discuss them. You may need to rephrase some questions if your learner struggles with their answer. Poor answers are often the result of poor questions. Be careful with the use of jargon; just because you understand it doesn't mean your learner will.

When asking questions, only use one question in a sentence, as more than one may confuse your learners and they might only answer the last one they heard. Try not to use questions such as 'Does that make sense?' or 'Do you understand?', as your learner will often say yes as they feel that's what you expect to hear. It doesn't tell you whether they have learnt or not. However, if you do, you could always follow this up with 'How does it make sense?' or 'What do you understand?'

If some learners don't feel comfortable answering questions in written format, perhaps due to a particular learning need, it might be possible to ask the questions orally and make a recording of the responses. You would need to find out if this is acceptable and, if so, under what conditions.

You will find more information regarding questioning in Chapter 3.

Holding discussions with your learner, often known as professional discussions
Professional discussions enable you to have a conversation with your learner based around the criteria being assessed. This is usually face to face but could take place via the telephone or the internet. However, it's not a question-and-answer session purely based on the criteria. The conversation should flow, and enable your learner to explain what they have done, with examples of how they have met the criteria. You will need to be careful how you word your questions and sentences, to be able to gain the responses you need. You will also need to keep a note of what was discussed, and/or record it as evidence of the conversation taking place. Professional discussions are useful to fill in any gaps which have not been met by another assessment method, or to ascertain responses to hypothetical situations.

Obtaining witness testimonies, for example from a learner's supervisor
It's useful to involve other people who work with your learner, for example their supervisor, who can give what's known as a witness testimony of their competence. You will need to liaise with them to confirm the authenticity of their statements. If witnesses are involved, they will need to be briefed as to what they are expected to do, and they must be familiar with the subject and criteria being assessed. You might also need to check a copy of the witness's curriculum vitae to confirm they are eligible.

Reading your learner's written statements of how they perform certain tasks
Learners can write their own statements of how they have achieved certain tasks to meet the criteria. You might also need to observe them and ask questions to confirm this. However, if you are not able to observe, perhaps due to confidentiality or safety reasons, your learner could write a statement and support this with a witness testimony and/or a visual or audio recording. The learner will need to be specific about what they have achieved. This is often called a *personal statement* instead of a written statement. Their supervisor could sign the statement to confirm what they have said is correct.

Learning journals are another way of a learner writing a statement. It's a useful method of ascertaining if a learner has put theory into practice. It will also show you how a learner writes, e.g. the structure of their sentences and use of grammar, spelling and punctuation. This will help confirm the work is that of the learner for authenticity purposes:

for example, if your learner normally speaks or writes in a different way from what is in their journal. If learning journals are used to make an assessment decision, it is beneficial to encourage the learner to cross-reference their writing to the criteria being assessed.

Recognising your learner's prior learning

Recognition of prior learning (RPL) is about assessing a learner's existing skills, knowledge and understanding towards what they are hoping to achieve. It should save them having to duplicate anything unnecessarily; however, it can be time-consuming to judge whether or not it meets the criteria. It could be that you have a learner who has achieved an aspect of a qualification or programme elsewhere. Depending upon the evidence they can produce in support of it, they might not have to repeat some or all of the learning again. You would need to compare what they have achieved already against the assessment requirements. You can then agree an assessment plan of how to fill the gaps: for example, by a discussion or an observation.

There are occasions where a learner will not have to repeat anything, particularly if they are taking a qualification and they have been accredited with some units already. This is known as an *equivalent unit*.

Example

> *Roberto had achieved the Inclusive Practice unit as part of the Certificate in Education and Training. His job role changed the following year and he decided to take the Diploma in Education and Training. As the Inclusive Practice unit was also in the Diploma, he did not have to retake it.*

There might be occasions where a learner will have an *exempt* qualification or unit. This means the qualification or unit is similar to the one being taken. There is therefore no need for a learner to take the newer version if the older version is still acceptable. Your learner will have a certificate from an awarding organisation to prove their achievement; however, you should always check the authenticity of these.

Example

> *Liang had achieved the Preparing to Teach in the Lifelong Learning Sector (PTLLS) qualification, which was replaced with the Award in Education and Training (AET). As the AET qualification was the revised version of PTLLS, he did not have to retake it.*

When claiming an equivalent or exempt unit towards a qualification, you will need to follow the awarding organisation's procedure, which might mean completing an RPL template. This role might be undertaken by someone else, rather than you, so you will need to liaise with them.

Assessment planning

Assessment planning should be both short term and long term, to allow *formative* (ongoing) and *summative* (at the end) assessment to take place. Including your learners in the assessment planning process will help identify what they have learnt already and what will be assessed, along with how and when they will be assessed. It will allow for communication to take place to clarify any points or concerns.

The assessment plan is like a written contract between you and your learner, towards the achievement of their qualification, standards, criteria, job role or whatever is to be assessed. Careful assessment planning and prior knowledge of your learner's previous achievements are the key to ensuring everyone involved understands what will take place and when. The plan can be reviewed and updated at any time to take into account progress as well as achievements. Rather than completing a separate feedback form when a learner has achieved something, the form could perform a dual function. Some organisations might use different documents which perform a similar role, such as individual learning plans (ILPs) or personal learning plans (PLPs).

Assessment planning should be specific, measurable, achievable, relevant and time bound (SMART).

- **S**pecific – the activity relates only to what is being assessed and is clearly stated.

- **M**easurable – the activity can be measured against the assessment requirements, allowing any gaps to be identified.

- **A**chievable – the activity can be achieved at the right level.

- **R**elevant – the activity is suitable and realistic, relates to what is being assessed and will give consistent results.

- **T**ime bound – target dates and times can be agreed.

Assessment planning should provide opportunities for both you and your learners to obtain and use information which is relevant to their progress and achievement. It should also be flexible and responsive; for example, by using technology. The way you plan should include strategies to ensure your learners understand what they are working towards, and the criteria that will be used for assessment. You should also plan how and when you will give feedback. It could be verbally, immediately after the assessment, or the next time you see your learner, or by email or other means. However, the sooner the better, while everything is fresh for both of you. Ideally, feedback should be given in a suitable and private environment. You will find more information regarding providing feedback in Chapter 4.

Assessment planning is a crucial part of the assessment process. If it is not carried out correctly and comprehensively, problems may occur which could disadvantage your learners and prevent them from being successful. When planning assessments, you will need to take into account equality of opportunity, inclusivity and differentiation within the assessment process. Never assume everything is fine just because your learners don't complain. Always include your learners in the assessment planning process in case there is something you don't know that you need to act upon.

Always ask your learners if there is anything you can do to help make their assessment experience a positive one. For example, ensure that you face your learners when speaking to assist anyone hard of hearing, or use written questions instead of asking oral questions (or vice versa) if necessary. If you use printed handouts make sure they are in a font, size and colour to suit any particular learner requirements.

Informal assessments will not require an assessment plan, such as role-plays and quizzes, if they are just to check ongoing progress. However, you must always be SMART when planning and using any formal assessment activities, to ensure they have a purpose.

Activity

Imagine you are going to be assessed demonstrating an aspect of your job role. What would you want to know beforehand? First, you would want to know why you are being assessed and who will be assessing you. You would then want to know what the assessor is looking for and how they will do it. You would also need to know when and where it will take place. This is known as an assessment rationale and will ensure the planning process and activities used are SMART. When planning assessments with your learners, you should use all these points.

Table 2.1 on page 34 an example of a completed assessment plan. However, assessment has not yet taken place, therefore feedback has not been given to the learner. Depending upon your organisation's requirements, and whether the forms will be completed manually or electronically, will determine whether or not signatures are also required. Feedback could be added to this form, or by using a separate feedback form, as in Table 4.2 in Chapter 4.

Assessment rationale

When planning to assess, you should have a rationale; you need to consider *who, what, when, where, why* and *how* (WWWWWH) assessment will take place. This information should always be agreed with your learner beforehand so that everyone is aware of what will occur. If you are assessing on an individual basis, the assessment planning process should still be formalised, and an assessment plan completed and agreed. When the assessment has taken place and feedback is given, or when you review your learner's progress, the plan can be updated.

Extension Activity

Consider the WWWWWH of the assessment planning process for your particular subject and, if possible, agree an assessment plan with a learner. Ensure you are familiar with the assessment criteria you will be assessing towards. Who else will you need to involve when creating the assessment plan (besides your learner)? What will you assess, when, where, why, and how will you do it?

Table 2.1 Example assessment plan and feedback record

Assessment plan and feedback record		
Learner: Irene Jones		**Assessor:** Jenny Smith
Qualification/unit: Level 1 Certificate in Hospitality & Catering (unit 101)		
Aspects to be assessed	**Assessment details**	**Target date**
101.3 Be able to help maintain a hygienic, safe and secure workplace.	An observation will take place on February 6th at the County Leisure Centre to assess competence in the work environment towards unit 101.3. The awarding organisation's observation form and checklist will be used for this purpose. A witness testimony will be obtained from Irene's supervisor. If any other aspects are seen during the observation which meet the criteria of other units, these will be taken into account.	6 February
101.4 Know how to maintain a hygienic, safe and secure workplace.	Oral questions and a discussion will take place to assess unit 101.4.	6 February
Feedback record		
Date	**Aspects assessed**	**Feedback**	**Action required**	**Target date**

Assessing vocational skills, knowledge and understanding

If you are not assessing competence in the work environment, you will probably be assessing an academic or a vocational programme which might lead to a qualification. You may also be teaching or training your learners, for example in a college or a training organisation. This would enable you to get to know your learners well before you assess them. Conversely, someone else might teach the learners and you might just be responsible for assessing them.

Examples of assessing vocational skills, knowledge and understanding include learners who are:

- attending English and maths programmes in an adult and community learning environment

- taking an employability programme in an offender institute or a prison

- attending a day release programme in a training organisation

- working towards a GCSE in a sixth-form college

- working towards an accredited qualification in a college or a training centre.

The subject you assess will determine the type and method of assessment to be used. For example, an academic programme could be assessed by an exam, whereas a vocational programme could be assessed by assignments. You will need to check the qualification specification, standards or criteria, to see what assessment activities are provided for you, or what you may have to devise to assess your subject. Table 2.7 later in this chapter lists various types of assessment, while Table 3.3 in Chapter 3 lists several methods of assessment.

Assessment activities can be initial (at the beginning), formative (partway through a programme), and/or summative (at the end of a unit, qualification or programme). Initial assessments will obtain information regarding your learner, and will help to identify a starting point and level. Formative assessments will check ongoing progress, and summative assessments will confirm achievement. Assessment activities can be assessor led (e.g. observations), or learner led (e.g. assignments), or a mixture of both. The methods you use will vary depending upon whether you are assessing skills, knowledge or understanding; some methods can cover both.

Assessment methods for vocational skills, knowledge and understanding

If you are assessing skills, knowledge and understanding, the most commonly used methods include:

- assignments, projects and/or case studies

- tests

- simulations.

Assignments, projects and/or case studies

You might need to create these assessment activities yourself, or they might be supplied by the awarding organisation if you are assessing an accredited qualification. You will need to make your questions very clear, as ambiguous or vague questions could confuse or mislead your learners. You also need to have a good idea of what you expect your learners to achieve so that you are fair when marking and assessing.

These types of activities can assess several areas of learning over time. A well-written project will help your learner provide evidence of knowledge and skills. This is known as holistic assessment as it assesses several aspects at the same time. If you are teaching as well as assessing, you will need to carefully plan the dates of issue and return. This will help with your own time management for marking and feedback, and ensure the work is equally distributed throughout the programme.

Tests

These might be theoretical or practical; they might be provided for you or you might have to create your own, for example, multiple-choice or short-answer questions. If you are marking written tests, you will need sample answers to compare with, to ensure you are fair to everyone. If you are part of a team of staff, you could create these together to aid consistency and standardisation.

If you are creating a test, make sure it is based around the criteria being assessed, and that appropriate learning has taken place. There's no point assessing if your learner isn't ready. Be careful how you administer any tests; you will probably use the same tests for different learners at different times, and therefore you need to ensure your learners have not seen each other's answers. You might need to administer a test formally, in timed and invigilated exam conditions. If you are unsure about this, ask someone you work with for guidance. Some tests will be marked externally by the awarding organisation or another assessor, and grades might also be allocated. An example of grading is when you give an A, B or C for a set number of correct responses, whereas marking judges whether a learner passes or not.

Simulations

A simulated activity can be assessed when it is not possible to observe something live: for example, assessing whether learners can successfully evacuate the building in case of a fire. You don't need to set fire to the building to observe this. Realistic working environments (RWEs) are often used in training centres to enable learners to work on real situations to put theory into practice. For example, brickwork learners might build a wall or plumbing learners might weld pipes. This will confirm that the learner can complete the task, but in a *realistic* rather than a *real* working environment. You will need to check the requirements of what is being assessed, to find out if simulation is acceptable or not.

Depending on what is being assessed, some activities can cover skills as well as knowledge and understanding, and can be assessed in the work environment. For example, a learner in a chemical plant could hold a discussion with their assessor about what actions would be taken in the event of a leak. This would cover the knowledge aspect; however, the under-standing and the skills would be demonstrated during a simulation or a real chemical leak.

Having the knowledge does not imply the understanding. For example, you know the earth is round, but do you understand why? When assessing knowledge, it might be enough for a learner just to know enough to get by, such as knowing certain historical dates. However, in other areas, understanding must be demonstrated as well as skills. You will find more information regarding assessment activities in Chapter 3.

When planning to carry out assessment activities, you will need to know when your learners are ready to be assessed. There's no point assessing them if they haven't learnt everything they need to know, as you will be setting them up to fail. If you don't teach as well as assess, you will need to communicate with the person who has taught the learner to ensure the required learning has taken place beforehand. If a learner has been absent for any reason, you will need to make sure they are up to date regarding what they have missed. Carrying out a formative assessment well before a summative assessment can help both you and your learner see how ready they are.

The timing of your assessments can also make a difference: if you plan to assess on a Friday before a holiday period, your learners might not be as attentive; equally so first thing on a Monday morning. This is difficult, of course, if you only see your learners on these particular days. If you are planning a schedule of assessments throughout the year, you will need to consider any public or cultural holidays. There is no point planning to assess on Mondays if the majority of these fall on public holidays.

Table 2.2 Skills, knowledge and understanding – assessment activities

Assessment activities to assess skills	Assessment activities to assess knowledge and understanding
• assignments (practical) • case studies (practical) • creating products, i.e. working models • peer assessment of an activity • observation of practical work in a laboratory, workshop or a realistic working environment (RWE) • projects (individual or team based) • recognition of prior learning (RPL) • self-assessment • simulations • skills tests • walk and talk	• assignments (theoretical) • case studies (theoretical) • discussions • examinations • presentations • projects (individual or team based) • puzzles and quizzes • recognition of prior learning (RPL) • reflective learning journals • role-plays • tests and multiple-choice questions • written and oral questions • written statements

Activity

If you haven't already done so, obtain a copy of the qualification specification or criteria you will be assessing for your subject. Ascertain what assessment activities have been provided for you, and what you need to create. When will you carry these out, i.e. on different dates for individual learners, or the same dates for groups of learners?

Action plans

You will need to carry out some form of action planning with your learners, even if it's just agreeing target dates for the submission of assignments, or planning ahead for the dates of tests or exams. Your learners will need to know what they are working towards, when they will be assessed, and how they will be assessed, for example, by assignments or tests.

This information could be in the form of an action plan rather than an assessment plan (see Table 2.3). The action plan would contain the details of the assignments or the expected test dates. It can be updated with achievement dates, and be added to or amended as necessary. Feedback could then be given separately as in Table 4.2 in Chapter 4.

Table 2.3 Example action plan

Action plan			
Learner: Marcia Indira		**Assessor:** Abbi Cross	
Qualification/unit: Level 2 Business, Administration and Finance (unit 1)			
Criteria	**Assignment questions**	**Target date**	**Achievement date**
Learning outcome 2	Q1 – Generate a range of ideas for a business enterprise	7 October	
Be able to develop a business enterprise idea.	Q2 – Compare the viability of the business enterprise ideas	14 October	
	Q3 – Select and develop a business idea	21 October	

If you are teaching as well as assessing, you will need to prepare a scheme of work to show what you will teach and when, and how you will assess skills, knowledge and understanding. A scheme of work is a document which outlines a sequence of sessions and what will be delivered and assessed during them. For example, formative assessments could include multiple-choice tests, questions, quizzes and role-plays which can assess progress. Summative assessments could include assignments, exams or tests to confirm achievement. When planning your programme delivery, make sure you have taught all the required material before carrying out any summative assessments. You will need to ensure appropriate time is planned for assessment activities during your sessions, or in between sessions, i.e. an assignment as homework. You will also need to plan adequate time for you to carry out marking and assessment, make a decision and give feedback to your learners. It's best to stagger the summative assessment activities so that you don't put too much pressure on your learners, or yourself, throughout the programme.

It could be that your learners will be taking an exam and this will need to be planned and invigilated, according to the awarding organisation's requirements, on a set date. Some assignments might also need to be completed under supervised conditions. You would therefore need to ensure that you have taught everything in good time. You could use past exam or test papers as a formative assessment activity to check the progress of your learners beforehand. This will also give them an idea of the structure that will need to be followed regarding their responses.

If your learners are working towards an accredited qualification, you will need to ensure they have been registered with the appropriate awarding organisation. It might not be your responsibility to carry out this task, but you should communicate the details of your learners to the relevant staff. If they have not been registered, the awarding organisation is not responsible for them and the results of assessments might be deemed invalid.

If a record of attendance or an in-house certificate will be issued to your learners upon successful completion, this information should be communicated to the person who will produce them. You should inform your learners when they can expect to receive any feedback or formal recognition of their achievements, and what they can do if they disagree with any decisions.

If you are responsible for devising your own assessment methods and activities, you might decide to choose ones which are easy to mark, for example multiple-choice questions. You might not have a lot of time for marking, therefore the more time you spend preparing something suitable and relevant, the easier the marking will be. There's no point making assessment activities complex unless it's a requirement of the qualification, or you need to challenge higher-level learners further. Conversely, lower-level learners can easily become demoralised if the activities are unattainable.

If you assess group work, such as presentations or role-plays, you need to assess each individual's contribution towards the assessment requirements. Otherwise you could be passing the whole group when some learners may not have contributed much at all. If you are related to, or know personally, the learners you will assess, you should notify your organisation of any conflict of interest. They may also need to notify the relevant awarding organisation in case you are not allowed to assess a learner if they are a partner, a relative, or a direct member of your family or your spouse's family.

Whatever subject you are going to assess, you need to ensure your learners have acquired and mastered the skills, knowledge, and understanding required at the right level for achievement. There's no point teaching your learners to repeat expected answers or to demonstrate a task if they don't really understand what they are doing and why.

Example

Isla had a group of learners working towards a qualification in desktop publishing. She had demonstrated how to carry out various functions on the computer and then asked them to work through past exam papers. The learners were soon able to pass all the papers; therefore they knew what they were doing, but did not understand why they were doing it that way. Consequently, when one of the learners got a job in desktop publishing, they were unable to perform their duties fully as they had only been taught to pass test papers.

Devising assessment materials

When you are devising assessment materials, such as assignments, essays or questions, you need to pitch these at the correct level for your learners. If you are assessing an accredited qualification, it will already be assigned a level; for example, Level 3 Certificate in Hospitality and Catering. If it's not accredited, you will need to pitch your assessment materials at the level which is appropriate for your learners: beginners, intermediate or advanced, or Level 1, 2 or 3. Knowing which level you are assessing towards will help you use the correct level of objectives when writing assessment materials.

Objectives

Objectives are represented by verbs, i.e. what you expect your learners to do, such as *analyse, describe* or *list*. To list would be at a lower level than to analyse.

Table 2.4 gives examples of objectives you could use when devising assessment activities at different levels. If you are assessing an accredited qualification, you will need to follow the objectives stated in the assessment criteria, which might be different from those in Table 2.4.

Bloom's taxonomy of learning

Bloom (1956) believed that education should focus on the mastery of subjects and the promotion of higher forms of thinking, rather than an approach which simply transfers facts. His *taxonomy model* of classification places learning into three overlapping *domains*. These are:

- the **cognitive** domain (intellectual capability, i.e. knowledge or thinking)

- the **affective** domain (feelings, emotions and behaviour, i.e. attitudes or beliefs)

- the **psychomotor** domain (manual and physical skills, i.e. actions or skills).

The three domains are summarised as *knowledge, attitudes and skills*, or *think, feel and do*. Your learners should benefit from the development of knowledge and intellect (cognitive domain); attitudes and beliefs (affective domain); and the ability to put physical skills into practice (psychomotor domain). You would therefore assess your learners at the right level for their learning, at the appropriate time, using the relevant domain.

Each domain contains objectives at different levels, such as *analyse, describe, explain* and *list*. You will see these objectives if you use a qualification specification for your subject; they are often referred to as *assessment criteria*.

Example

Pierre has a group of learners working towards a Level 1 Certificate in Engineering. He carries out formative assessment of his learners using objectives such as state (to test knowledge), familiarise (to test attitudes), and use (to test skills). When he is sure his learners have mastered the topics, he will give them a summative test which will assess the required knowledge, attitudes and skills needed to achieve the unit from the qualification.

If Pierre used objectives such as *justify* and *facilitate*, these would be too high a level for his learners to achieve. If his learners progress to Level 2, Pierre could then use objectives relevant to that level, such as *describe* and *demonstrate*.

Table 2.4 Examples of objectives at different levels

Level	Skills		Knowledge and understanding		Attitudes	
Foundation	Attempt Carry out Learn Listen Read		Answer Match Recall Repeat Show		Adopt Assume Contribute Listen	
1	Arrange Help Imitate Obtain	Switch Use View Watch	Access Know List Locate	Name Recap Recognise State	Adapt Co-operate Familiarise	
2	Assist Change Choose Connect Demonstrate Draw	Perform Practise Prepare Present Rearrange	Compare Describe Identify Reorder Select Write		Accept Consider Develop Express Question Understand	
3	Apply Assemble Assess Build Create Construct Design	Devise Estimate Facilitate Illustrate Make Measure Produce	Compose Explain Paraphrase Test		Appreciate Challenge Defend Determine Discriminate Enable	Participate Predict Relate Review Study Visualise
4	Calculate Complete Convert Diagnose Explore Generate Maintain	Modify Plan Quality assure Research Search Solve	Analyse Invent Contextualise Outline Revise Summarise Verify		Appraise Command Criticise Debate Define Discuss Influence	Judge Justify Persuade Rationalise Reflect
5	Accept responsibility Encapsulate Establish	Interview Manage Organise Teach	Categorise Classify Contrast Evaluate Interpret		Argue Critically appraise Define	Differentiate Dispute Formulate Suggest
6	Operate Utilise		Extrapolate Synthesise Translate		Conclude Hypothesise Justifiably argue	
7	Modify		Strategise		Critically differentiate	
8	Lead		Redefine		Critically discriminate	

(Note: Some might occur or be repeated at different levels depending upon what is being assessed.)

If a qualification is offered at different levels, often the learning outcomes are the same, but the assessment criteria are different. The latter might use objectives such as *describe* for a lower level, *explain* for an intermediate level and *analyse* for a higher level. The content of the qualification remains the same; the difference is in the amount of work the learners will do to achieve a higher level. However, learners will often feel they are capable of achieving a higher level, even though that might not be the case.

Example

Elaine is assessing the Equality and Diversity unit. She has a mixed group of Level 3 and Level 4 learners. All of the learners opt to take the Level 4 assessments. However, once Elaine assesses their responses, she realises most of them only meet the criteria for Level 3. When she informs them of this, they do not take the feedback well.

In this example, all the learners felt they were capable of a higher level of achievement, and were therefore demoralised when told they did not meet the requirements. If an initial assessment had been carried out, the learners would have been aware of their abilities and which level to work towards.

If you have a mixed group of learners, to aid differentiation, you could adapt your formative assessment activities to reflect what *everyone* should achieve, what *most* will achieve and what *some* will achieve. For example, everyone will *describe*, most will *explain* and some will *analyse*. This is a useful way of challenging more able learners while those less able can still achieve something.

Extension Activity

Design three different assessment activities which you could use with your learners. They should be based around the criteria you are going to assess and be at the correct level. You should create example responses for any questions that you are asking. This will help when marking and will ensure consistent, valid and reliable assessment decisions. If possible, carry out the activities with your learners and evaluate their strengths and limitations.

Types of assessment

Different subjects will require different *types* of assessment, for example *formal* tests or *informal* role-plays. Formal assessments are to confirm achievement and are usually planned and carried out according to the assessment requirements or criteria. Informal assessments can occur at any time to check ongoing progress. Assessment types are different to assessment methods. The method is how the type will be used. For example, an informal *type* of assessment would be by using the *method* of questioning a learner during a review of their progress. Table 2.5 gives examples of assessment methods which are formal and informal. Table 2.7 later in the chapter contains a comprehensive list of types of assessment, along with their descriptions.

Table 2.5 Formal and informal assessment methods

Formal	Informal
• assignments • case studies • essays • examinations • multiple-choice questions • observations • professional discussions • projects • recognition of prior learning • reviewing learner evidence • tests • witness testimonies • written questions	• crosswords • discussions • gapped handouts (sentences with missing words) • journals/diaries • peer and self-assessment • puzzles • practical activities • questions: oral, written, multiple choice • quizzes • role-plays • worksheets

(Note: Some can occur in both depending upon the situation.)

Five frequently used assessment types are:

• initial

• diagnostic

• formative

• summative

• holistic.

Initial assessment

Using initial assessments will help you to find out about your learners, and identify any particular aspects which might otherwise go unnoticed. It's best to do this prior to the programme commencing. This will allow time to deal with any issues that might arise, or to guide learners to a different, more appropriate programme if necessary. Some organisations might use a *training needs analysis* (TNA) in place of or in addition to an initial assessment. Using a TNA can identify current skills and knowledge with a view to planning further training and assessment. Initial assessment can also be used at the beginning of a new unit or module to ascertain previous and current skills, knowledge and understanding.

Initial assessment can:

• allow for differentiation and individual requirements to be planned for and met

• ascertain why your learner wants to take the programme along with their capability to achieve

• find out the expectations and motivations of your learner

- give your learner the confidence to negotiate suitable targets

- identify any information which needs to be shared with colleagues

- identify any specific additional support needs.

Example

Jennifer had applied to take a Conflict Management qualification and was attending an interview with the trainer. After discussing her current skills and knowledge, and her aspirations for using the qualification to improve her career, she decided it wasn't for her. She felt she lacked confidence; therefore the trainer referred her to the National Careers Service where she could get further advice.

Table 2.6 Example initial and diagnostic assessment template

Initial and diagnostic assessment *Separate tests in English, maths and ICT should be taken.*		
Name:	Date:	
What experience do you have in this subject area?		
What relevant qualifications do you have?		
Have you completed a learning preference questionnaire? If YES, what is your preferred style of learning? If NO, please complete the questionnaire at www.vark-learn.com and note your results here:	YES/NO Learning preference results: V: A: R: K:	
Do you have any particular learning needs or requirements? If YES, please state here, or talk to your assessor in confidence.	YES/NO	
Are you confident at using a computer? If YES, what experience or qualifications do you have?	YES/NO	Test results: ICT:
What help would you like help with written/spoken English?		Test results: English:
What help would you like help with maths?		Test results: Maths:
Why have you decided to take this programme/qualification?		

Diagnostic assessment

Diagnostic assessments can be used to evaluate a learner's skills, knowledge, strengths and areas for development in a particular subject area. It could be that your learner feels they are capable of achieving at a higher level than the diagnostic assessments determine. The results will give a thorough indication of not only the level at which your learner needs to be placed for their subject, but also which specific aspects they need to improve on. Skills tests can be used for learners to demonstrate what they can do; knowledge tests can be used for learners to demonstrate what they know and understand.

Diagnostic tests can also be used to ascertain information regarding English, maths, and information and communication technology (ICT) skills. Information gained from these tests will help you plan to meet any individual needs and/or to arrange further training and support if necessary. Diagnostic assessments can be used as part of the information, advice and guidance service (IAG) if applicable.

Diagnostic assessment can:

- ascertain learning preferences, e.g. *visual, aural, read/write* and *kinaesthetic* (VARK)
- enable learners to demonstrate their current level of skills, knowledge and understanding
- ensure learners can access appropriate support
- identify an appropriate starting point and level for each learner
- identify gaps in skills, knowledge and understanding to highlight areas to work on
- identify previous experience, knowledge, achievements and transferable skills
- identify specific requirements, for example; English, maths and ICT skills.

Activity

Find out what initial and diagnostic assessments are used at your organisation. Will it be your responsibility to administer these, or is there a specialist person to do this? If possible, carry out an initial and/or diagnostic assessment with a learner. How will you use the results to help plan what your learner will do and when?

There are many different types of initial and diagnostic tests available. Some organisations design and use their own; others purchase and use widely available tests, such as the system called *Basic Key Skills Builder* (BKSB) to diagnose English, maths and information and communication technology (ICT) skills.

The results of initial and diagnostic assessments should help you negotiate appropriate assessment plans with your learners, ensuring they are on the right programme at the right level with the support they need to succeed.

It could be that your learner has achieved some units of a qualification elsewhere and might just need to provide their certificate as evidence of prior achievement.

Example

Sarah had completed a diagnostic assessment process which was designed to assess her skills and knowledge towards the Level 2 Diploma in Travel and Tourism. Sarah had started the qualification at another organisation prior to moving to the area. Her current assessor was able to see her evidence for three units which she had recently completed. Sarah was therefore accredited with these units once her assessor had confirmed all the requirements had been met. She therefore did not need to be reassessed.

Once you have the information you need from the initial and diagnostic assessment process, you can agree an assessment plan with your learner. The template in Table 2.6 opposite is a form which could be used or adapted for initial and diagnostic assessment purposes. It should be supported with appropriate skills tests for English, maths and ICT.

Formative assessment

Formative assessments should take place continually throughout your learners' time with you. These are usually carried out informally to review progress, identify any support requirements and inform further development. Simply asking questions and observing actions can help you assess how your learners are progressing. You could use activities, quizzes and short tasks for them to carry out which would make the assessment process more interesting, and highlight any areas which need further development.

Summative assessment

Summative assessments usually occur at the end of a session, programme, topic, unit or full qualification. They are a measure of achievement towards set requirements or criteria rather than focusing on progress. This type of assessment can often be quite stressful to learners and sometimes leads to a fail result even though the learner is quite capable under other circumstances. If you are assessing a programme where the activities are provided for you, such as examinations or tests, there is often a tendency to teach purely what is required to achieve a pass. Teaching to pass examinations or tests does not maximise a learner's ability and potential. They might be able to answer the questions just by relying on memory. This doesn't help them in life and work, as they might not be able to put theory into practice afterwards, or even understand what they have learnt.

Summative assessment is usually formal, devised by the awarding organisation that accredits the qualification, and is often called assessment *of* learning as it counts towards the achievement of something.

Holistic assessment

Learners might be able to demonstrate several criteria from different aspects or units at the same time. These can therefore be assessed together, known as *holistic* assessment. You may be able to observe naturally occurring situations in addition to what has originally been planned. For example, if you are watching a learner perform a task, they may also do something which had not been planned for, but which occurred during the activity. Don't discount this because it wasn't planned, but inform your learner that you were able to assess them for these other aspects at the same time.

Rather than planning to assess individual aspects or units on different occasions, you could discuss your learner's job role with them to identify which criteria from other areas could be demonstrated at the same time. You could also involve the learner's supervisor (if applicable) as they might be aware of situations where the learner can demonstrate their competence. While the assessment might take longer, it would reduce the number of assessment activities and therefore the inconvenience to all involved. Your learner would need to be ready to demonstrate their competence; don't plan to assess unless they are. Never arrange to assess your learner if they are not ready, as this could demoralise them and waste time. Holistic assessment should make evidence collection and demonstration of competence much more efficient.

Holistic assessment is beneficial to all concerned when assessing occupational competence, particularly in a work environment. It could be that you carry out a holistic assessment and find your learner is competent according to most but not all of the criteria you planned to assess. If this is the case, you can still sign off what they have achieved and then update the assessment plan to assess against the remaining criteria on another occasion. Alternatively, you might be able to ask questions or hold a discussion with your learner to evidence the gaps, if this is acceptable. If so, you would need to keep a record of what was asked, and the responses your learner gave. Without records, there's no proof of what has occurred.

Using different types and methods of assessment

You will probably use different types and methods of assessment methods depending upon whether you are assessing knowledge or performance. Knowledge is usually assessed by assignments, essays and tests. Performance is usually assessed by observations, questions and discussions. However, these will vary depending upon the subject you are assessing and where you are assessing. Formal assessment activities are usually provided by the awarding organisation (if you are assessing an accredited qualification). You should be able to devise your own informal methods to check ongoing progress with your learners.

All assessment types and methods should be suitable to the level of your learners. A Level 1 learner might struggle to maintain a journal of their progress and a Level 2 learner may not be mature enough to accept peer feedback. A Level 3 learner may feel a puzzle is too easy, and so on. Some learners may respond better to informal assessment rather than formal assessment. You need to consider the assessment requirements for your subject, and how you can best implement these, without changing the assessment criteria.

Example

Laura sees her group of learners once a week for an Art and Design programme. Each week, she commences the session by asking some questions regarding the topics covered in the previous week. This is informal formative assessment to check progress. Towards the end of term, she will issue an assignment. This is formal summative assessment to confirm their achievement.

You might have all the details of types and methods of assessment provided for you; if not, you will need to carefully select these to suit your subject, the situation and your learners. You might decide to assess your learners on a formative basis throughout their time with you to check progress, and use a summative test at the end to confirm achievement. This would enable you to see how they are progressing, and whether or not they will be ready for the formal assessment. You might be provided with tests or assignments for your learners to complete at set times during the programme. To be sure your learners are ready you could use activities, quizzes and smaller tasks for them to carry out beforehand. This would make the assessment process more interesting and highlight any areas that need further development. If you are assessing a programme whereby the activities are provided for you, for example tests or exams, there is often the tendency to teach purely what is required to achieve a pass. Learners may therefore not gain valuable additional skills and knowledge. Teaching to pass tests does not maximise a learners' ability and potential.

Extension Activity

Look at Table 2.7 and choose four types of assessment that you could use with your learners. Devise some assessment materials based on them for your particular subject. If possible, use them and then evaluate how effective they were, and what you would do differently next time.

Table 2.7 Types of assessment

Types of assessment	Description
Academic	Assessment of theory, knowledge and/or understanding.
Adaptive	Questions are selected during a test on the basis of their difficulty, in response to an estimate of the learner's ability.

Types of assessment	Description
Analytic scoring	A method of scoring grades for tests such as speaking and writing. For example, a writing test would have an analytic score based on grammar and vocabulary.
Aptitude	A diagnostic test to assess a learner's ability for a particular skill, job or vocation.
Assessor led	Assessment is planned and carried out by the assessor: for example, an observation.
Benchmarking	A way of evaluating learner performance against an accepted standard. Once a benchmark standard is set, it can be used as a basis for the expectation of achievements with other groups/learners.
Blended	Using more than one assessment method in different contexts: for example, observation in the work environment backed up with online knowledge assessments in a training room.
Competence based	Assessment methods are based on certain criteria that learners need to perform in a workshop or work environment.
Controlled assessment	An activity or test which occurs in a number of stages with varying levels of control to ensure reliability. Ensures the same conditions for everyone and is usually timed.
Criterion referencing	Assessing prescribed aspects which a learner must achieve to meet a certain standard, sometimes referred to as assessment criteria.
Diagnostic	A specific assessment relating to a particular topic or subject and level, which builds on initial assessment. It is sometimes called a skills test. The results determine what needs to be learnt or assessed in order to progress further. Some types of diagnostic assessments can also identify learners with dyslexia, dyspraxia, dysgraphia, dyscalculia and other learning difficulties.
Differentiated	Adapting an informal assessment activity to suit a learner's abilities and needs. Permission might be required from an awarding organisation for adaptations to formal assessment activities.
Direct	Evidence provided by a learner to meet the requirements being assessed: for example, products from their work environment.
Evidence	Learners provide examples of products or written statements to prove their competence and knowledge towards agreed criteria.
External	Assessments set and marked externally by an awarding organisation.
Formal	Assessment that involves the recognition and recording of achievement, often leading to certification of an accredited qualification.
Formative	Ongoing, interim or continuous assessment to determine progress; for example, an observation. Can be used to assess skills and/or knowledge in a progressive way, to build on topics learnt and to plan future learning and assessments. Often referred to as assessment *for* learning, allowing additional learning to take place prior to further assessments.

(Continued)

Table 2.7 (Continued)

Types of assessment	Description
Holistic	Assessing several aspects of a unit, qualification, standards, criteria, programme, or job specification at the same time.
Independent	An aspect which is assessed by someone other than the designated assessor.
Indirect	Evidence provided by others regarding a learner's progress: for example, a witness testimony from their supervisor at work.
Informal	Assessment that is in addition to formal assessment to measure progress: for example, questioning during a progress review.
Initial	Assessment at the beginning of a programme or unit, relating to the subject being learnt and assessed, to identify a learner's starting point and level. Initial assessment can also include diagnostic assessments to ascertain the results of learning preferences, and English, maths and ICT tests. The latter can be used as a basis to help and support learners.
Integrated	A way of linking and assessing theory and practice. Information acquired in a learning context is put into practice and assessed in a work environment.
Internal	Assessments carried out within an organisation, either internally set and marked, or externally set by an awarding organisation or professional body and then internally marked.
Ipsative	A process of self-assessment to recognise development. Learners match their own achievements against a set of standards or their own previous achievements. This is useful for learners to consider how they are progressing. However, they do need to work autonomously and be honest with themselves.
Learner led	Learners plan how they can achieve what is required, and then produce evidence of this. The learner informs the assessor when they are ready to be formally assessed, having self-assessed their work first.
Linear	Assessment takes place at the end of a programme of learning.
Modular	Assessment takes place after a module or unit of learning.
Norm-referencing	Comparing the results of learner achievements to each other: for example, setting a pass mark to ensure a certain percentage of a group will achieve.
Objective	Based around the criteria being assessed, which does not lead to a personal opinion of the learner or the learning.
Predictive	An indication of how well the results from a test or activity will predict future performance.
Process	The assessment of routine skills or techniques: for example, to ensure a learner is following a set process or procedure.
Product	The outcome is assessed, but not the process of making or working towards it: for example, a completed painting or an operational model.

Types of assessment	Description
Proficiency	An assessment to test ability or skills without reference to any specific programme of learning: for example, riding a bicycle.
Profiling	A way of recording learner achievements for each individual aspect of an assessment. Checklists can be a useful way to evidence these and more than one assessor can be involved in the process.
Psychometric	A test of psychological qualities, for example intelligence and personality.
Qualitative	Assessment is based upon individual responses to open questions given to learners. Clear criteria must be stated for the assessor to make a decision, as questions can be vague or misinterpreted.
Quantitative	Assessment is based upon yes/no or true/false responses, agree/disagree statements, or multiple-choice tests, giving a clear right or wrong answer. Totals can be added to give results: for example 8 out of 10. Learners could pass purely by guessing the correct answers; however, computer-generated questions are often formulated to minimise this.
Screening	A process to determine if a learner has a particular need, for example in English or maths.
Subjective	A personal decision by the assessor, where the assessment criteria might not have been clearly stated. This can be unfair to a learner.
Summative	Assessment at the end of a unit or programme to determine achievement, for example an exam. If a learner does not pass, they will usually be offered another chance. Often known as assessment *of* learning, as it shows what has been achieved at a given point.
Triangulation	Using three assessment methods: for example, observation, oral questioning and a test. This helps ensure the reliability and authenticity of a learner's work and makes the assessment process more interesting.
Vocational	Job-related practical assessment, usually in a learner's work environment.

Supporting learners

At some point, you might have a learner who requires specialist support. Your role might require you to support your learners in some way, for example with personal or welfare aspects as well as professional and learning aspects. Some learners may have barriers, challenges or needs that could affect their attendance and/or progress and achievement. Hopefully, you can ascertain these prior to your learners commencing, perhaps from their application form or through the initial assessment process. However, some learner needs may become evident during the programme and you would need to plan a suitable course of action to help them, or refer them to an appropriate specialist or agency. If you can be proactive and notice potential needs before they become issues, you might be able to alleviate your learner's concerns. Otherwise, you will need to be reactive to the situation and deal with it professionally and sensitively.

Some examples of meeting your learners' needs include:

- adapting or providing resources and equipment for a learner who is partially sighted

- adapting the environment for a learner who is physically disabled

- allowing extra time for a learner with dyslexia or dyscalculia

- arranging to use another language such as British Sign Language with a learner who is partially deaf

- changing an observation date and/or time for a learner who works shifts

- liaising with others who could offer advice regarding financial concerns

- providing specialist support staff to improve English and maths skills

- providing the assessment information in an alternative format, such as spoken, instead of written for a learner who has impaired vision

- using a different location which is more accessible to learners who have to travel far

- using different assessment activities to suit individual learning preferences

- using new and emerging technologies to help improve confidence with ICT skills

- using larger print, Braille, or other alternative support mechanisms for learners with particular needs.

You may feel you can deal with some of these yourself; however, you should always refer your learners to an appropriate specialist or agency if you can't. Never feel you have to solve any learner issues yourself and don't get personally involved; always remain professional.

Learning support and learner support

If you have a learner requiring support for any reason, there is a difference between *learning support* and *learner support*. Learning support relates to the subject, or help with English, maths or ICT skills. Learner support relates to any help your learner might need with personal issues, and/or general advice and guidance regarding their health, safety and welfare.

Always ask your learners how you can support them, but try to avoid making them feel different or uncomfortable. If you are unsure of what you can do to help your learners, ask someone at your organisation. The Equality Act (2010) requires organisations to make reasonable adjustments where necessary. Don't assume you are on your own to carry out any amendment to provision; there should be specialist staff to help.

When planning assessments, you need to consider any particular requirements of your learners, to ensure they can all participate. Initial assessment would ensure your learners are able to take the subject; however, you (or the organisation) may need to make reasonable adjustments to adapt resources, equipment or the environment to support them. If anything is adapted, make sure both you and your learners are familiar with the changes prior to carrying out the assessment activity. You might not be able to change the criteria against which you are assessing, but you can change the way you implement the assessment process. If you need to make any changes, you must consult the relevant awarding organisation to discuss these if the qualification is accredited. Most will have an Access to Assessment policy which will inform you of what you can and cannot do. You cannot change a set examination date and time without approval, and you may need consent in writing for other changes or amendments to assessments.

Activity

Think about your learners and the environment in which you will be assessing. Do you need to ask your learners if any adaptations or changes are required? Will the timing of the assessments impact on your learners in any way: for example, during an evening session when they may not have had time to eat? Find out what you are allowed to amend in accordance with the requirements. Check what documentation and guidance are available to support learner needs.

All learners should have equality of opportunity and appropriate support to enable them to access assessment. It could be that you don't need to make any special arrangements just yet, but knowing what to do, and who to go to, will make things easier for you when such circumstances do occur.

Some learners may lack self-confidence, or have previous experiences of assessment that were not very positive. Many factors can affect a learner's motivation; therefore you need to ensure you treat all your learners as individuals, using their names, and making the assessment experience interesting and meaningful to them. Some learners may need more attention than others. Just because one learner is progressing well doesn't mean you can focus on those that aren't; all your learners need encouragement and feedback. You may not be able to change the environment or the resources you are using, but remaining professional and making the best use of what you have will help encourage your learners' development.

Example

Frank has a group of learners working towards GCSE geography. One of his learners, Joanna, seems to be losing motivation and is not paying attention during sessions. As Frank knows she enjoys working with computers, he arranges for the class to move to the computer room to use a specialist website which has GCSE online activities for learners to complete. These give immediate scores, which will help Frank monitor his learners' progress, and help retain the motivation of Joanna and the group.

You need to encourage your learners to reach their full potential. If you use assessment activities that are too difficult, learners may struggle and become frustrated and anxious. If assessments are too easy, learners may become bored. Knowing your learners and differentiating for their needs should address the balance.

If you have learners who are quite motivated already, keep this motivation alive with regular challenges and constructive feedback. A lack of motivation can lead to disruption and apathy. If you are teaching as well as assessing, ensure you are reaching all learning preferences, as everyone learns differently. For example, learners might be predominantly *visual*, *aural*, *read/write* or *kinaesthetic* (VARK). This will help you plan suitable assessment activities or modify your methods of assessment if appropriate. You might not be able to change the formal assessments required, but you could devise informal assessments which will help motivate and suit your learners' needs.

Example

Gill had always assessed her learners by assignments and tests. After encouraging them to complete a learning preference questionnaire at www.vark-learn. com, she realised several of her learners prefer a kinaesthetic approach. She has therefore changed some of her informal assessments to include role-play and practical activities which will meet their learning preferences.

Using the correct type of assessment to suit your learners, carrying out careful and appropriate assessment planning, and reviewing progress will ensure you are meeting the needs of your learners. You will also make sure your learners are on the right pathway to achieving a successful result and that you are differentiating for any individual requirements.

Barriers to assessment

Some learners may have barriers to assessment such as health problems, or a lack of access to a particular room, or transport issues. You may have to challenge your own values and beliefs if you don't agree with those of your learners, to ensure you remain professional at all times. Other learners may have a support assistant who will be present during the assessment process. They will be there to help your learner in case they have any difficulties. Make sure you address your learner, not their assistant, to ensure you are including them fully in the process. For example, if you have a learner with a speech impediment, give them time to finish speaking before continuing.

Your organisation should have support mechanisms to meet any special assessment requirements or individual needs of learners, for example a learner services department. If this is not the case, you will need to find out who can provide advice and guidance when needed.

Examples of support for learners include:

- **Dyspraxia** – allow additional time and space if necessary for learners who have poor motor co-ordination.

- **Dysgraphia** – allow the use of a computer or other suitable media for learners who have difficulty with handwriting.

- **Dyscalculia** – allow additional time if necessary and use calculators or other equipment for learners who have difficulty with calculations or maths.

- **Dyslexia** – allow additional time or resources if necessary for learners who have difficulty processing language. Present written questions in a simplified format, such as bullet points. Ask questions verbally and make an audio or visual recording of your learner's responses; allow the use of a laptop for typing responses rather than expecting handwritten responses.

- **A physical or mental disability** – learners could be assessed in a comfortable environment where appropriate access and support systems are available. Learners could be given extra time to complete the assessment tasks, or to take medication privately. Dates could be rearranged to fit around doctor or hospital appointments.

- **A hearing impairment** – an induction loop could be used where all or part of an assessment is presented orally. Instructions and questions could be conveyed using sign language. Specialist computer software could be used.

- **A visual impairment** – use large print or Braille, use specialist computer software if available, ask questions verbally and make an audio recording of your learner's responses.

- **Varying work patterns** – try to schedule the assessment at a time and place to suit.

- **English as a second or other language** – if allowed, try to arrange assessments in your learner's first language. Many awarding organisations can translate assessment materials if requested. Bilingual assessments should also be offered if required.

Example

If you have a learner who has dyslexia, it may be appropriate to ask questions rather than give a written test, or to have someone to note their responses. For a learner who is partially sighted you could give papers in a larger font or use a magnified reading lamp. For a learner who is deaf, you could give a written test instead of an oral test. For a learner with Asperger's syndrome, you could use written questions rather than oral questions. For some learners who might struggle with spelling and grammar, the use of a computer could help. An adapted keyboard or a pen grip could help a learner who has arthritis.

Safeguarding

Safeguarding is a term used to refer to the duties and responsibilities which those providing a health, social or education service have to perform to protect individuals and vulnerable people from harm. Following the introduction of the Safeguarding Vulnerable Groups Act in 2006, a vetting and barring (VB) scheme was established in autumn 2008. As an assessor, you will be bound by this Act if you work with children (those under the age of 18 years and in training) and/or vulnerable adults. You might be required to have a criminal record check via the Disclosure and Barring Service (DBS) before you can work as an assessor. You might also need to attend safeguarding training every three years (some staff every two years depending upon their safeguarding involvement).

A vulnerable adult is defined as a person aged 18 years or over, who is in receipt of or may be in need of community care services by reason of 'mental or other disability, age or illness and who is or may be unable to take care of him or herself, or unable to protect him or herself against significant harm or exploitation' (Bonnerjea, 2009, p. 9).

This could be anyone needing formal help to live in society, such as a young mother, someone with a learning disability or a recently released prisoner. If your organisation is inspected by Ofsted, it will be asking your learners how safe they feel and whether they are able to give you feedback regarding any concerns they may have.

You have a duty of care and a personal responsibility towards all your learners and should apply six key elements of appropriate service provision:

- respect
- dignity
- independence
- individuality
- choice
- confidentiality.

There are four key processes that should be followed to ensure your learners are safe:

- an assessment of their needs
- planning services to meet these needs
- intervention if necessary when you have a concern
- reviewing the services offered.

If you have any concerns regarding a learner, for example if you feel they are being bullied, or at risk of radicalisation, harm or abuse, you must do something. You should talk to someone immediately, such as a designated safeguarding officer (DSO) or your supervisor. There should also be a 'prevent duty' in place for those at risk of radicalisation. This is required under the Counter-Terrorism and Security Act (2015). Never be tempted to get personally involved with your learner's situation.

Health and safety

Your role as an assessor will require you to follow various regulations, one of which is the Health and Safety at Work etc. Act (1974). This places a legal responsibility upon you as well as your organisation and your learners. If you see a potential hazard, it is your responsibility to do something about it before an accident occurs, even if this is just reporting it to the relevant person within your organisation. The health and safety of yourself, your colleagues and your learners is of paramount importance.

You might have to carry out a risk assessment to ensure the area and assessment activities are safe for all concerned. It can normally be achieved by a walk-through of the area, and a discussion with those involved. However, a formal record must be kept in case of any incidents. You probably unconsciously carry out a risk assessment whenever you do anything: for example, when crossing the road, you would automatically check the traffic flow before stepping out.

Equality and diversity

All learners should have equality of opportunity throughout the assessment process, providing they are taking a programme they are capable of achieving. There's no point setting learners up to fail, just because you need a certain number of learners for your programme to go ahead, perhaps due to targets or funding. When designing and using assessment activities, you need to ensure you meet the needs of all your learners and reflect the diverse nature of your group. Never let your own attitudes, values and beliefs interfere with the assessment process. You could design activities which will challenge more able learners and/or promote the motivation of learners who are not progressing so well. You need to differentiate your activities to ensure you are meeting the needs of all your learners, perhaps using less challenging activities for those who are struggling. However, you will need to check what you can adapt to ensure you are not changing the assessment criteria.

The *National Occupational Standards for Learning and Development* (2010) give the following definitions of equality and diversity:

Equality – A state of fair treatment that is the right of all people regardless of difference in, for example, culture, ability, gender, race, religion, wealth, sexual orientation, or any other group characteristic.

Diversity – Acknowledging that each individual is unique, and recognising our individual differences in, for example, culture, ability, gender, race, religion, wealth, sexual orientation, or any other group characteristic. (LLUK, 2010, p. 35)

Your organisation should have an Equality and Diversity or Equal Opportunities policy with which you should become familiar. You might have a learner who achieves tasks quickly; having more in-depth and challenging activities available would be beneficial to them. If you have learners who are not achieving the required assessment tasks, you could design an activity which you know they will achieve, to raise their motivation and encourage them to progress further. However, don't oversimplify activities, which will leave learners thinking they were too easy. You could give your learners a choice of a straightforward, a challenging, or a very challenging activity. Their choice may depend upon their confidence level and you will have to devise such activities beforehand if they are not provided for you. If you have different levels of learners within the same group, this can work quite well as they will usually want to attempt something they know they can achieve. However, it can also have the opposite effect, in that learners feel they are more capable than they actually are. These types of activities are more suited for formative assessment which checks progress. You might need to arrange assessments in other languages for those for whom English is not their first language, for example Polish or Welsh, or use a bilingual approach if necessary.

Assessment activities should always reflect the diverse nature of your learner group, for example, culture, language and ethnicity. They should not be biased according to the person producing them, otherwise aspects such as terminology or jargon might not be those of the learners, but those of the producer, placing the learner at a disadvantage. You also need to be careful not to discriminate against a learner in any way.

The Equality Act (2010) replaced all previous anti-discrimination legislation and consolidated it into one Act (for England, Scotland and Wales). It provides rights for people not to be discriminated against or harassed: for example because they have an association with a disabled person or are wrongly perceived as disabled. In this instance, reasonable adjustments must take place during assessment activities to lessen or remove the effects of a disadvantage to a learner with a disability.

The Act contains nine *protected characteristics*:

- age
- disability
- gender reassignment
- marriage and civil partnership
- pregnancy and maternity
- race
- religion or belief
- sex
- sexual orientation

There are seven different types of discrimination:

- **Associative discrimination** – direct discrimination against someone because they are associated with another person with a protected characteristic.
- **Direct discrimination** – discrimination because of a protected characteristic.
- **Indirect discrimination** – when a rule or policy which applies to everyone can disadvantage a person with a protected characteristic.
- **Discrimination by perception** – direct discrimination against someone because others think they have a protected characteristic.
- **Harassment** – behaviour deemed offensive by the recipient.
- **Harassment by a third party** – the harassment of staff or others by people not directly employed by an organisation, such as an external consultant or visitor.
- **Victimisation** – discrimination against someone because they made or supported a complaint under equality legislation.

It is important to take the protected characteristics into account when planning and carrying out assessment activities, and to ensure discrimination does not take place by anyone involved in the assessment process. Try and focus on the positive and always ask what your learner *can* do, not what they *can't* do.

Further details regarding equality and diversity can be found in the book *Equality and Diversity in the Lifelong Learning Sector* (Gravells and Simpson, 2012).

Extension Activity

Find out what the procedures are at your organisation for supporting learners. How can you support them should you identify any challenges or barriers to assessment, or any particular learning needs?

Summary

Knowing how to plan for assessment in different contexts will ensure the activities you use with your learners are valid and reliable. Understanding the different types of assessment, such as initial, formative and summative, will help you plan appropriate activities to use with your learners at the right time. Ascertaining any barriers to learning and minimising the risks involved will help you support your learners appropriately throughout their time with you.

You might like to carry out further research by accessing the books and websites listed at the end of this chapter.

This chapter has covered the following topics:

- Assessing occupational competence in the work environment
- Assessing vocational skills, knowledge and understanding
- Types of assessment
- Supporting learners

References and further information

Bloom, B. S. (1956) *Taxonomy of Educational Objectives: The Classification of Educational Goals*. New York: McKay.

Bonnerjea, L. (2009) *Safeguarding Adults: Report on the Consultation on the Review of 'No Secrets'*. London: Department of Health.

Coffield, F. (2008) *Just Suppose Teaching and Learning Became the First Priority*. London: Learning and Skills Network.

Department for Education and Skills (DfES) (2006) *Safeguarding Children and Safer Recruitment in Education*. London: DfES.

Gravells, A. and Simpson, S. (2012) *Equality and Diversity in the Lifelong Learning Sector* (2nd edn). Exeter: Learning Matters.

LLUK (2010) *The National Occupational Standards for Learning and Development.* London: Lifelong Learning UK.

Race, P., Brown, S. and Smith, B. (2004) *500 Tips on Assessment.* Abingdon: Routledge.

Read, H. (2011) *The Best Assessor's Guide.* Bideford: Read On Publications.

Read, H. (2013) *The Best Initial Assessment Guide.* Bideford: Read On Publications.

Olin, R. and Tucker, J. (2012) *The Vocational Assessor Handbook* (5th edn). London: Kogan Page.

Wolf, A. (2008) Looking for the best result. *Make the Grade*, Summer. Institute of Educational Assessors.

Websites

Assessment resources – **www.excellencegateway.org.uk** and **www.questionmark.co.uk**

Basic Key Skills Builder – **www.bksb.co.uk**

Counter-Terrorism and Security Act (2015) – **www.legislation.gov.uk/ukpga/2015/6/contents/ enacted**

COSHH – **www.hse.gov.uk/coshh**

Disability and the Equality Act – **http://tinyurl.com/2vzd5j**

Disclosure and Barring Service – **www.gov.uk/government/organisations/disclosure-and- barring-service/about**

Equality and Human Rights Commission – **www.equalityhumanrights.com**

Health and Safety Executive – **www.hse.gov.uk**

Health and safety resources – **www.hse.gov.uk/services/education/information.htm**

Diagnostic assessment: assessing the need for dyslexia support – **http://rwp.excellencegateway. org.uk/Diagnostic%20Assessment/Support%20for%20dyslexia/**

Initial assessments for Functional Skills English and maths – **http://qualifications.pearson.com/en/ qualifications/edexcel-functional-skills/teaching-support/initial-assessment-tool.html**

Initial assessments for ICT – **www.tes.co.uk/teaching-resource/ict-initial- assessments-6177727**

Learning preferences – **www.vark-learn.com**

Literacy diagnostic assessment materials – **http://rwp.excellencegateway.org.uk/ Diagnostic%20Assessment/Literacy/**

National Careers Service – **https://nationalcareersservice.direct.gov.uk**

Numeracy diagnostic assessment materials – **http://rwp.excellencegateway.org.uk/ Diagnostic%20Assessment/Numeracy/**

Office safety and risk assessments – **www.officesafety.co.uk**

Prevent duty and safeguarding resources – **www.preventforfeandtraining.org.uk**

Support for adult learners – **www.direct.gov.uk/adultlearning**

Training needs analysis – **www.businessballs.com/trainingneedsanalysis.pdf**

Introduction

There should always be a reason for any assessment activity you carry out. The main reason is to check if learning has taken place. The results of assessments will help to identify what your learner has achieved, whether they are ready to progress further, and what they need to do next. There are many methods of assessment and activities you could use, depending upon what you are assessing and where. Using a mixture of different ones will help make the assessment process more interesting, stimulating and motivating for both you and your learner.

This chapter will explore the different methods of assessment you can use with your learners, including those which involve technology, along with the risks involved when assessing learning.

This chapter will cover the following topics:

- Methods of assessment
- The role of technology in assessment
- Questioning techniques
- Minimising risks

Methods of assessment

Assessment can only take place once learning has occurred, but how do you know that this has happened? You might be able to answer this by saying, 'I'll ask some questions', or 'I'll observe my learner performing a task'. That might be all right if you know what questions to ask and how your learner should respond, or what you expect to see. However, to assess effectively, you will need to plan ahead and use appropriate methods of assessment when you know your learners are ready.

To effectively plan how you will assess your learners, besides adhering to the principles covered in Chapter 1, you will need to use methods which are ethical, fair and safe.

- **Ethical** – the methods used are right and proper for what is being assessed and the context of assessment. The learner's welfare, health, safety and security are not compromised.

- **Fair** – the methods used are appropriate to all learners at the required level, taking into account any particular needs. All learners should have an equal chance of an accurate assessment decision.

- **Safe** – the learner's work can be confirmed as valid and authentic. There should be little chance of plagiarism; confidentiality of information should be taken into account; learning and assessment should not be compromised in any way, nor the learner's experience or potential to achieve. (Safe in this context does not relate to health and safety but to whether the assessment methods are sufficiently robust to make a reliable decision.)

Example

If you give your learners the information to answer questions, this is unethical. If you give some learners more help than others, this is unfair. If you allow your learners to copy text from the internet to answer questions without quoting their source, it will be deemed unsafe.

There are several different assessment methods you could use, for example observations, questioning, tests and exams. If assessment activities are not provided for you, you will need to devise your own. Always take into account a learner's needs, the level of achievement they are aiming for, and the subject requirements, before planning to use any assessment activities. The methods you choose will depend upon what you will assess, where and how. Table 3.3 at the end of this chapter lists several methods of assessment, approaches and activities you could use, along with a brief description, and their strengths and limitations.

Never be afraid to try something different, particularly with formative assessments that you can design yourself. Formative assessments check progress, whereas summative assessments check achievement. You could use puzzles, quizzes or crosswords as a fun and active way of informally assessing progress. You could try searching the internet for free software to help you create some activities; a few sites are listed at the end of this chapter. You could even try letting your learners design their own assessment activities if appropriate. This would help them analyse what is to be assessed and devise suitable ways this can be achieved. You could use peer assessment as part of the process. You would still have the final say regarding whether or not your learners have met the requirements.

When using any activity, you need to ensure it is inclusive, and differentiates for any individual needs, learning difficulties and/or disabilities (LDD). Always follow health and safety guidelines, and carry out any relevant risk assessments where applicable. Make sure your learners are aware of why they are being assessed, and don't overcomplicate your activities by using too many at the same time.

Peer assessment and self-assessment

Peer assessment involves a learner assessing another learner's progress. Self-assessment involves a learner assessing their own progress. Both methods encourage learners to make decisions about what has been learnt so far, take responsibility for their learning, and become involved with the assessment process. This approach gives your learners responsibility in the assessment *for*, and *of* their learning. Assessment *for* learning involves finding out a starting point for future learning and assessment. Assessment *of* learning involves making a decision regarding what has been learnt so far.

Your learners will need to fully understand what needs to be assessed, and how to be fair and objective with their decisions and any feedback given. Throughout the process of peer and self-assessment, learners can develop skills such as listening, observing and questioning. However, the results of peer and self-assessment are not usually counted towards meeting the requirements of a qualification, as you should make the final decision regarding achievement. However, in the workplace, peer-assessment might be counted as proof the learner has met the requirements of a job role, for example, if the peer is a colleague of the learner. Table 3.1 on page 64 gives the advantages and limitations of peer and self-assessment.

Peer assessment

Peer assessment involves a learner assessing another learner's progress. This would actively involve your learners during a session. However, you would need to ensure everyone was aware of the criteria being used, how to reach a decision and how to give constructive feedback.

> *This assessment method requires a good level of self-criticism and personal awareness and may need to be 'taught' before embarking on as a reliable method of assessment ... Authenticity is the main risk associated with this method of assessment in that candidates may not be familiar with the units of competence or be as confident in deciding sufficiency. (Wilson, 2012, p. 49)*

Peer assessment can be a useful way to develop and motivate learners. However, this should be managed carefully, as you may have some learners who do not get along and might use the opportunity to demoralise one another. You would need to give advice to your learners as to how to give feedback effectively. If learner feedback is given skilfully, other learners may think more about what their peers have said than about what you have said. If you believe peer assessment has a valuable contribution to make to the assessment process, ensure that you plan for it, to enable your learners to become accustomed and more proficient at giving it.

Peer feedback could be written down rather than given verbally, and will therefore be anonymous. This would encourage objective opinions as learners will not feel they are betraying their peers. Ground rules should be established, such as the way feedback will be structured and given, to ensure the process is valid and fair. If feedback will be written anonymously, your learners must be aware that using harsh or demoralising comments could have a negative and detrimental effect.

Examples of peer assessment activities include:

- assessing each other's work and giving written or verbal feedback
- giving grades and/or written or verbal feedback regarding peer presentations and activities
- holding group discussions before collectively agreeing a grade and giving feedback, perhaps regarding a learner's presentation
- suggesting improvements to their peers' work
- producing a written statement of how their peers could improve and/or develop their practice in certain areas.

Table 3.1 Advantages and limitations of peer and self-assessment

Peer assessment advantages	Peer assessment limitations
• helps develop communication skills • leads to discussions from which everyone can benefit • learners are focused upon the assessment requirements or can refer to a checklist • learners may accept comments from peers more readily than those from the assessor • peers might notice something the assessor hasn't • promotes attention as learners have to focus on what is happening • increases attention for activities such as peer presentations if feedback has to be given • promotes learner and peer interaction and involvement	• all peers should be involved, therefore planning needs to take place as to who will give feedback, to whom and in what order • appropriate conditions and environment are needed • the assessor needs to confirm each learner's progress and achievements, as it might be different from their peers' judgements • everyone needs to understand the assessment requirements • learners might be subjective and friendly rather than objective with their decisions • needs to be carefully managed to avoid personality conflicts or unjustified comments • should be supported with other assessment methods • some peers may be anxious, nervous or lack confidence to give feedback
Self-assessment advantages	**Self-assessment limitations**
• encourages learners to check their own progress • encourages reflection • mistakes can be seen as opportunities • promotes learner involvement and personal responsibility • learners are focused upon the assessment requirements • learners can identify when they are ready for a formal assessment • learners take ownership of the process, i.e. identifying areas for improvement	• the assessor needs to discuss and confirm progress and achievement • difficult to be objective when making a decision • learners may feel they have achieved more than they actually have • learners must fully understand the assessment requirements • learners need to be specific about what they have achieved and what they need to do to complete any gaps • some learners may lack confidence in their ability to make decisions about their own progress

Boud (1995) suggests that learning and development will not occur without self-assessment and reflection. However, this must be done honestly and realistically if it is going to aid improvement. This process can promote learner involvement and personal responsibility. All learners should be fully aware of the requirements of what is being assessed, and therefore ensure that their work is focused towards meeting it.

Self-assessment

Self-assessment involves a learner assessing their own progress, which can lead to them appreciating what they have achieved and what they need to do. It can give responsibility and ownership of their progress and achievements. However, learners might feel they have achieved more than they actually have; therefore you will still need to confirm their achievements or otherwise.

Examples of self-assessment activities include:

- awarding a grade for a presentation they have delivered

- suggesting improvements regarding their skills and knowledge

- compiling a written statement of what they could do differently or how they could improve their work.

Activity

Design two activities to use with your learners based on peer assessment and self-assessment. Use the activities and analyse how effective they were. What would you change and why?

Portfolios of evidence

Some qualifications require learners to produce a portfolio of evidence which you will need to assess. A portfolio is a file or folder of documents and information, known as *evidence*, which proves achievement, and can be stored manually or electronically. It is an ideal opportunity for learners to holistically cross-reference the evidence they provide across several areas, such as units of a qualification or aspects of a job description. There is no need for them to produce a separate piece of evidence for all the individual assessment criteria; they can just give the evidence a reference number and quote this number against the other relevant assessment criteria it meets. If this is the case, your learner should have a copy of the assessment requirements to help them understand what is required. You can both refer to this when planning the types of evidence which will be provided, and how and when you will assess it.

Portfolios usually contain:

- a record of achievement or summary, i.e. a list of what has been achieved along with dates and signatures

- assessment plans and feedback records

- an authentication statement by the learner that all the work is their own

- written statements by the learner as to how the evidence meets the criteria

- the learner's evidence cross-referenced to the criteria

- any other documents, such as witness testimonies, to support the learner's achievements.

With any portfolio, the quality of the evidence is important, not the quantity. When you are assessing evidence, you don't want to be spending a lot of time searching for something, and neither will anyone else, for example an internal quality assurer. Some qualifications might require you, as the assessor, to cross-reference the evidence rather than the learner. However, enabling your learner to do it gives them ownership of what they have done. You should plan what is required and by when, encouraging your learner to self-assess their evidence towards the relevant assessment criteria before giving it to you. Learners could also provide evidence towards other aspects which have not been planned for. For example, if they are submitting evidence towards Unit 1, but find it also covers Unit 2, this should still be submitted and assessed. Always give a copy of your assessment records to your learners as proof that the assessment process took place, and of the decisions made. The originals should be kept according to your organisation's procedures.

Electronic portfolios

Electronic portfolios, known as *e-portfolios*, are becoming more popular as learners can generate and upload their evidence to an online system. Often the assessment criteria are already within the online system and will enable the learner to cross-reference their evidence when uploading. They can also keep track of their progress and achievements. Some systems also allow communication to take place between assessors and learners and track all contact. Evidence can be in the form of data files, scanned documents, videos, digital and audio files. Assessment of evidence can therefore take place remotely. Your assessment records and feedback can also be uploaded to, and managed through, the system. Assessment in the form of an observation might still be necessary, although this could be digitally recorded and/or observed via a web camera. When assessing electronic evidence, you must make sure that it has been produced solely by your learner, who might have to show you photo identification at some point. If you are ever in doubt as to whether the learner is who they say they are, you will need to follow your organisation's procedure to ascertain this.

The use of e-portfolios might not suit every learner and every qualification. You might find some learners will use a manual system, some an electronic system and others might use both. You should differentiate the process to suit your learners, what is being assessed and the programme they are working towards.

The positive aspects of using e-portfolios include the following:

- They are accessible from work, home and mobile devices at any time.

- As an assessor, you become familiar with the style in which the learner writes; not only the tone and language, but the font style and size, therefore it becomes easy to notice any anomalies and spot plagiarism.

- Audio, video or photographic evidence can often be uploaded straight from a mobile phone to an e-portfolio.

- The problem of the learner forgetting to bring their portfolio to an assessment is eliminated.

- It encourages learners to take ownership of their portfolios as they can decide which assessment criteria they believe their evidence covers.

- Learners often have to add a description to the evidence they're uploading and this in itself can provide further evidence, i.e. if a learner uploads evidence of performance, when describing it they are also demonstrating their knowledge.

- There is no need to transport heavy portfolios between assessment sites.

- On some systems, the feedback you provide is automatically linked to the assessment criteria, which can be very time-saving.

- The learner can provide links to other websites where their work can be found: for example they might have a blog, Instagram account or YouTube channel, or they might have produced work which is on their organisation's website.

- The learner cannot lose their e-portfolio, so evidence and assessment records are less likely to be lost.

- The learner's e-portfolio might also be available to their line manager: for example, if they are taking a qualification in the workplace, their line manager can upload witness testimonies to provide evidence about the learner's performance.

- The units are pre-populated with the assessment criteria which learners can access from the start of their programme.

- There is usually a function which shows when all users last accessed the system, so you know if your learners have been active.

- Transparency – the quality assurers can log on and sample learner evidence and assessment records.

The negative aspects of using e-portfolios are:

- All e-portfolio systems are different and there is no one ideal system.

- E-portfolio systems can be unnecessarily complicated in their format, with feedback and action plans being stored in a separate area to the units and evidence. It's important to show your learners where the feedback and action plans are saved.

- If undertaking a workplace observation, very often you will have to leave the premises to upload your observation and feedback record, as your own device might not connect to the organisation's network.

- Learners are able to edit and delete evidence, which means that following developmental feedback they might edit an existing piece of evidence rather than add new evidence. This might not be obvious to the assessor and therefore could be missed.

- Learners are not assessors, so it's important for assessors to check which assessment criteria the learner has claimed they have met. Often it covers far more when assessed holistically against all the units, but it might not cover everything the learner thinks it does.

- Learners can sometimes be overwhelmed by having access to all the assessment criteria from the start of their programme, as they can see the sheer volume of work that needs to be completed.

- Learners can try to claim that the system malfunctioned and deleted all the work that they uploaded (when actually they haven't done anything).

- Maximum uploadable file sizes can be incredibly small; for example, if you have made a digital recording of your learner in action, it might need to be stored elsewhere if it exceeds the maximum file size.

- The message system within an e-portfolio often allows you to send a message to a learner's email account, but it won't allow the learner to reply directly. They have to log into the e-portfolio, which removes the immediacy and accessibility of responding to feedback and action points.

- The system can time out or malfunction, which can cause problems when uploading evidence.

- While work stored on the e-portfolio system is safe (subject to your organisation maintaining a subscription to the provider), work saved on social media platforms such as Instagram or YouTube is owned by the provider. This poses a risk, however small, that the provider could remove the work or close down the site, resulting in all work being lost.

Extension Activity

Think about the learners you have at present, or those you will be assessing in the future. How do you know that learning has taken place? Look at Table 3.3 at the end of this chapter, choose four methods and create an activity for each. If possible, use them with your learners and analyse how effective they were. What would you change and why?

The role of technology in assessment

Technology is constantly evolving and new resources are frequently becoming available. It's crucial to keep up to date with new developments and you should try to incorporate these within the assessment process. *Digital literacy* denotes the use of and benefit from information and communication technology (ICT), which can be a useful tool for learning and assessment. However, never assume your learners are capable or confident at using ICT; always carry out an initial assessment to ascertain their skills, knowledge and understanding. They, and indeed you, might need some training first, for example how to access, log on and use a particular program. The use of technology can also assist when differentiating assessment activities to meet a particular learner's requirements, such as a screen reader or text enlargement software for a learner who is partially sighted. *Assistive* or *adaptive technology* denotes devices and their use for people with disabilities or difficulties. It can lead to greater independence by providing enhancements to or changing the methods of use. This should enable learners to accomplish tasks they might not have been able to do without it.

There should be a code of practice for the use of ICT for both staff and learners to follow. You will need to locate and read this and ensure that your learners are familiar with it. For example, if learners are using programs via the internet during a session, they should not be accessing their own social media. Following the code and agreeing some ground rules will help ensure that the use of technology is reasonable and safe.

E-learning, short for *electronic learning*, includes the use of both learning and assessment technologies: for example, data projectors, interactive whiteboards, virtual learning environments (VLEs) and the teaching, learning and assessment methods that they encompass. If someone is learning in a way that uses any information and communication technologies, i.e. computers and other equipment, software and online applications, then they are using e-learning. The FELTAG report *Paths forward to a digital future for Further Education and Skills* (2014) recommends an increase in the use of technology (10 per cent of learning to be online) and for students to take responsibility for their own learning. If the programme you deliver and assess does not incorporate the use of technology, you could encourage your learners to access and use it in their own time. *Open education resources* (OER) are digital resources which are uploaded, exchanged and shared by teachers and assessors online. If you carry out a search for a topic you are planning to deliver and/or assess, you will probably find lots of sites with resources you can use. You might need to register with the site first, or reciprocate by uploading a resource of your own before downloading another. Please see the website list at the end of this chapter for examples of sites which could be accessed by both you and your learners.

You need to establish what technology is available for your own and your learners' use, and what support is available. You may be assessing in an environment which has access to all types of technology and technical support, for example wi-fi enabled computers, digital recording equipment, devices such as tablets and smart phones. However, do you know if support would be available at the times you might need it, if a technical problem occurred? If you are making a visual or audio recording of your learners, in any environment, you would need to find out if this is acceptable, and if so under what conditions. This could include obtaining permissions from others who might appear in the recording.

There might be a *learning resource centre* (LRC) or library within your organisation, or a public library which is accessible locally. They are no longer places which just contain books; many have computers connected to the internet, photocopying facilities, and other resources such as journals, magazines, newspapers and periodicals (manual and electronic). If there is an LRC or library at your organisation, you could arrange for a member of the team to give your learners a short tour of the facilities.

Technology can be accessed via different devices and used in different environments. For example:

- *Open environments (such as social networks/media, discussion forums/boards and anywhere else freely accessible on the Web) – the content can be seen, shared, commented upon by anyone.*

- *Closed/restricted environments (such as groups, networks and media where membership is by invite only or is shared with only a selected community/audience. Parts of virtual learning environments (VLEs), such as group work activities can be thought of in this way) – the content is only available to invited or registered users.*

- *Private/personal environments (such as email accounts, personal storage in the cloud, personal areas of institutional portals and VLEs) – the environment and its content is only available to you. You may be able to customise the environment and possibly communicate or share some content with others through it. (White, 2015, p. 31)*

If you have computer and internet facilities in the learning environment, do make use of them whenever possible. However, never make assumptions about technology and whether it is accessible or in working order. Always check the equipment personally and in the context in which you are planning to use it. Have a contingency plan in case of technical failure. If it's at all possible, request that assistance from technical support staff be available if you are using something for the first time.

Encouraging your learners to use technology will help increase their skills in this area. Technology can be combined with traditional methods of teaching and assessment; this is known as *blended learning.* For example, after a training session, learners could complete an assessment activity online via the VLE. You can then give feedback via email or the VLE system. Learners can communicate with each other and you through the VLE chat room, which could be asynchronous (taking place at different times) or synchronous (taking place at the same time). Combining methods also promotes differentiation and inclusivity.

Technologies in common use include:

- blogs, chat rooms, social networking sites, webinars and online discussion forums to help learners communicate with each other

- computer programs and applications for learners to produce their assignments and save documents and pictures

- cloud storage facilities that learners and assessors can use to upload and access materials from various devices

- digital media for visual/audio recording and playback

- electronic portfolios for learners to store their work

- email for electronic submission of assessments, communication and informal feedback on progress

- interactive whiteboards for learners to use for presentations and to display their work

- internet access for research to support assignments or presentations

- mobile phones and tablets for taking pictures, video and audio clips, and communicating with others

- networked systems to allow access to applications and documents from any computer linked to the system

- online and on-demand tests which can give instant results: for example, diagnostic, learning preferences and multiple-choice tests

- online discussion forums which allow asynchronous (taking place at different times) and synchronous (taking place at the same time) discussions

- scanners for copying and transferring documents to a computer

- web cameras or video conferencing if you can't be in the same place as your learners and you need to see and talk to them

- VLEs to access and upload learning materials and assessment activities.

Example

Jacqui had always been reluctant to use technology during her Beauty Therapy sessions with learners. However, as she had a new group of learners who all had their own mobile devices, she felt she should incorporate their use for formative assessment. She created an online quiz based on the topic of the session, which her learners were able to access on their own devices. They completed the quiz individually and then compared their results in pairs. The activity went well and Jacqui decided to create more formative assessment activities to upload to the VLE. Her learners could access these outside the normal learning environment to support their progress.

Social media

Social media focuses on building networks or social relationships among people who share interests and/or activities. Social media is software that allows learners to communicate based around an idea or topic of interest. Popular tools are Facebook, Twitter and LinkedIn, which are used worldwide. A social network service consists of a profile for each user (name, interests, etc.), their social links, and a variety of additional services. Most social network services are web based and provide a means for users to interact via the internet, such as talking to others who are accepted and trusted by the user.

Activity

Access the internet and have a look at various social media sites such as Facebook, Twitter and LinkedIn. You could join them and use them for professional networking and communication. Be careful of revealing anything personal about yourself as it will remain accessible for a very long time. You could also look at using cloud-based storage sites such as Dropbox, Pinterest and YouTube. These sites are ideal to upload materials for your learners to access in their own time.

You could use social media sites to encourage your learners to communicate and engage in discussions, and to support each other outside the learning environment. Learning should reflect the world and society of today, which includes working in virtual social environments. You may need to train your learners how to be effective collaborators, how to interact with people around them, how to be engaged and informed and how to stay safe in the virtual world.

Bring your own device (BYOD) is the term for learners using their own devices for learning and assessment (ground rules should be established).

Learners need to be aware of the powerful ways social media can change the way in which they look at education, not just their social lives. You need to promote the incredible power of social-networking technology which can be used for academic benefits. It could be called *academic networking* rather than *social networking*. Anyone with a device and an internet connection could set up and use the facility.

Example

From the author of Digital Literacy Skills for FE Teachers (2015 p. 17). His experience of IT education made him realise how much people's needs from such courses have changed over time:

- *In the late 1990s I undertook a short CLAIT course at an FE College while studying my A Levels. The course was covered using computers for tasks relevant to everyday life and work, such as understanding the main features of a Microsoft Windows-based computer, using word-processing software to type and print letters and entering data into spreadsheets in order to produce graphs and charts. At the time we were told that skills in these packages were sufficient skills for most home and work-based tasks.*

- *By 2005, when I was running IT workshops for the public, there was very little interest in learning about word processing and spreadsheet software. Session attendees instead wanted to know how to set up and use email accounts, buy and sell on Ebay and how to upload and manipulate their digital photographs. This was a clear change, from people wanting IT training in order to computerise the paper-based tasks they did, to people wanting IT training to enable them to do new things and change their habits.*

- *In 2015, our needs for IT training have evolved and changed again, with people now wanting to know how to choose, set up and manage a variety of online accounts (e.g. social media accounts, cloud-based storage accounts and communication service accounts); advice on making decisions on which devices to purchase/discard and what benefits each has over the other (e.g. PCs, laptops, smartphones, tablets); to know how to present themselves professionally online and apply for jobs and other opportunities; help with linking together and managing all the digital devices in their home, in order to share files, music, photos and video with ease (e.g. WiFi routers, smart TVs, wireless printers, wireless audio systems).*

Table 3.2 **Advantages and limitations of using technology**

Advantages	Limitations
• accessible and inclusive • address sustainability, i.e. no need for paper copies • an efficient use of time and are cost-effective, i.e. eliminates time taken to travel to individual assessment sites • auditable and reliable • available, i.e. resources and materials can be accessed at a time and place to suit • give immediate results from online tests • learners can 'bring your own device' (BYOD) to use during sessions • on demand, i.e. tests can be taken when a learner is ready	• finance is required to purchase or upgrade equipment • it can lead to plagiarism via the internet • it is time-consuming initially to set up • it might create barriers if learners cannot access, or are not confident to use, technology/the internet • learners accessing sites via their own devices might run out of credit • power cuts/low broadband speeds/limited network of wi-fi coverage could cause problems • security of data could be compromised • some learners might be afraid of using new technology • some organisations block access to certain sites and social media • there might not be enough resources available for all learners to use at the same time (if part of group work)

Online assessment

Online assessment (electronic assessment, or e-assessment) can be used in addition to other assessment methods. For example, learners could complete a multiple-choice test which will automatically be marked and give instant results. The system could generate different questions for each learner so that no two tests are the same. Tests can be undertaken on demand when a learner is ready and can take place anywhere there is a suitable device with access to the software. However, supervision might be necessary for some online tests and feedback via the system might be meaningless.

There are some programmes which are only delivered and assessed online. If this is your role, it's possible you will never meet your learners in person. Online programmes enable learners and assessors to upload a photo and add a profile of themselves, and this helps everyone to get to know each other. You will need to build up a rapport with your learners but do not become too friendly or too personal in case you cross the boundaries of your professional role. Online programmes allow communication to take place in real time, for example during live online chats, or not in real time, for example by taking part in discussion forums where responses can be added later.

The essential elements of being an e-assessor are:

- **Accessibility and availability** – being able to log on and respond to learners' postings in an engaging and encouraging way.

- **Communication** – posting regular forum messages and chats to encourage communication which is clear and concise (with minimal use of jargon), interaction and the sharing of good practice between all. Setting the scene for learners with a clear introduction and the requirements of the course, along with expectations for successful completion. Giving timely feedback regarding progress and achievement.

- **Enthusiasm** – confidence with ICT and motivation to apply the role and support the learning process.

- **Knowledge** – of the online system and the subject being assessed.

If you are delivering online training as well as assessing, it could be that you are not familiar with the learning/assessment materials if they have been produced by someone else. Therefore you might want to work through them first, in case you are asked any questions about them by your learners. If you create any materials, make sure your instructions are clear; don't assume your learners will understand what you are asking them. Read everything you create from a learner's perspective. If you are an online assessor, you might not be involved in any training with your learners, but just assess their work and give feedback. If this is the case, you still need to get to know your learners, as this will help you when assessing that their work is authentic. For example, if you know how your learner responds in the discussion forums, but their writing is very different when answering formal questions, then you might be concerned the work is not their own.

The key issues of online assessment are:

- availability and access to the software or applications being used, familiarity with ICT, internet availability and download speeds

- encouraging learners to update their profiles, agree a social etiquette and communicate with others within the online community

- ensuring learners are fully aware of what they need to do, along with target dates

- ensuring the authenticity, safety and security of learners' work and data

- knowing when to intervene or moderate in a situation that might become out of hand: for example, issues not related to the subject

- moderators and quality assurers might require to see hard copies of learners' work and assessors' feedback, for example if the qualification is accredited via an awarding organisation

- motivating learners to establish a routine, for example to commit regular times for study, online communication and discussions, and the submission of work

- being aware that screen sizes differ, therefore some people might struggle to read on a small screen

- the support each individual will require

- time management for the planning of synchronous learning and communication to take place in real time.

If you want your learners to work together as part of an online community, it's important to carry out an icebreaker, agree some ground rules and encourage them to interact with each other and yourself. Good interpersonal skills, approachability, enthusiasm and a strong commitment to the programme will help you establish and maintain motivation and interaction.

Some online programmes can have hundreds of learners; they are called MOOCs, which stands for **M**assive **O**pen **O**nline **C**ourses. These are often open to anyone who is interested in a particular subject which is offered, and who has an internet connection. The downside of this for an assessor is that the number of learners allocated to them will vary; many learners tend to drop out, and a lot of time might be needed to manage the learning process effectively.

E-learning and e-assessment are constantly advancing. Unfortunately, there isn't room in this book to explain it in great detail, so please refer to other appropriate texts and websites such as those listed at the end of this chapter.

Extension Activity

Create a new resource for your subject using ICT. This could be an activity for learners to collaborate on via cloud computing, a computerised presentation, or a video or podcast. Choose something that makes you feel excited about using it and consider how it will inspire and motivate your learners. Use the activity with your learners and then evaluate how effective it was. What changes would you make and why?

Questioning techniques

Questions are a really useful method of formative assessment to ensure your learners are acquiring the necessary knowledge and understanding before moving on to a new topic. They can also be used as summative assessment at the end of a programme, for example, in a test or exam.

Questions can be verbal or written, and can be *open*, requiring a full answer, or *closed*, requiring a 'yes' or 'no' answer. If you are asking questions verbally to a group of learners, ensure that you include all the learners. Don't just let the keen learners answer first, as this gives the ones who don't know the answers the chance to stay quiet. Tell your learners you are going to use a particular method before you ask questions. For example, pose a question, pause for a second and then pick a learner to answer the question. This way, all learners are thinking about the answer as soon as you have posed the question, and are ready to speak if their name is called. This is sometimes referred to as *pose, pause, pick* (PPP). If you use this process, make sure you have enough questions for everyone in the group so that no one is left out. If your nominated learner doesn't know the answer, ask them to guess. That way they still have to think and can't opt out. If they still don't know, say they made a good attempt and then move on to another learner.

To ensure you include everyone throughout your session, you could have a list of their names handy and tick each one off after you have asked them a question. This is fine if you don't have a large group. If you do, make sure you ask different learners each time you are in contact with them. When asking questions, only use one question in a sentence, as more than one may confuse your learners. Try not to ask, 'Does anyone have any questions?', as often only those who are keen or confident will ask, and this doesn't tell you what your learners have learnt. Try not to use questions such as 'Does that make sense?' or 'Do you understand?', as your learners will often say yes as they feel that's what you expect to hear, or they don't want to embarrass themselves. However, if you find yourself doing this, follow it up by asking *why* it makes sense, or *how* they understand it.

When questioning:

- Allow enough time for your questions and your learner's responses.

- Ask open questions, i.e. those beginning with *who, what, when, where, why* and *how*.

- Avoid trick or complex questions.

- Be aware of your posture, gestures and body language.

- Be conscious of your dialect, accent, pitch and tone of voice.

- Don't ask more than one question in the same sentence.

- Generate activity and energy when using closed questions to a group by asking learners to stand up, then ask them to sit down for a *yes* answer (or vice versa).

- Know that some learners might be shy, therefore direct your questions to a table of learners (if you have groups) to help encourage their input.

- Make sure you don't use closed questions to illicit a *yes* response too often; learners may feel that is what you want to hear but it doesn't confirm their understanding.

- Use active listening skills to show you are concentrating on hearing what they have to say.

- Try not to say *erm, yeah, okay, you know,* or *does that make sense?*

- Try not to use a lot of jargon.

- Use eye contact when talking to an individual learner or, as you ask a question to a group, by alternating looking at each learner for a second as you speak.

- Use learners' names when possible.

- Watch your learners' reactions and body language.

Activity

Look at the bullet list above and ask yourself if you do them all. If there are some that you don't, how can you improve the way you ask questions?

Whenever possible, try to use open questions which require an answer to demonstrate understanding, rather than closed questions which only give a yes/no answer. The latter doesn't show you if your learner has the required knowledge as they could make a correct guess by accident. Open questions usually begin with who, what, when, where, why and how.

If you are having a conversation with your learner there are some other questioning techniques you can use, such as probing, prompting, clarifying, leading, hypothetical, reflective, and rhetorical, as well as open and closed questions. Some questioning techniques are better than others, and it will take practice to use the ones which are most effective for your particular learners.

Example

Open: 'How would you . . . ?'

Closed: 'Would you . . . ?'

Probing: 'Why exactly was that?'

Prompting: 'What about . . . ?'

Clarifying: 'Can you go over that again?'

Leading: 'So what you are saying is . . .'

Hypothetical: 'What would you do if . . . ?'

Reflective: 'If you could do that again, how would you approach it?'

Rhetorical: 'Isn't that a great display that Peter has put together for his practical assignment?'

Rhetorical questions are good for engaging your learner in conversation, but they usually only require your learner to agree or disagree with you. They should be followed up with another type of question to elicit knowledge.

When asking questions verbally, make sure you allow enough time for your learner to answer. Skilful questioning should be matched with skilful listening to ensure you understand what is being said. Be careful of your body language and tone of voice when asking questions, and try not to use a lot of jargon.

If there are no clear guidelines or assessment criteria for you to base your questions on, you might find yourself being *subjective* rather than *objective*. That is, you make your own decision without any guidance and therefore base it on your opinion rather than on fact. It is harder to remain objective when learners are responding to open questions which do not have any clear assessment criteria to follow, or any expected response as a guide.

If you produce written questions for your learners to answer, think how you will do this, i.e. short questions, essay-style questions with word counts, open, closed or multiple-choice. If you are giving grades (e.g. A, B, C, or pass/merit/distinction), you must have clear grading criteria to follow to make sure your decisions are objective, in the event that your learners might challenge your decisions.

Example

Haedish has a group of learners who need to achieve at least 8 out of 10 to achieve a pass. The questions have been written by a team of staff within the organisation, but no expected responses have been provided. Haedish has been told to use her professional judgement to make a decision, but finds this difficult. She knows her learners are very capable of achieving, but they don't always express themselves clearly when writing. She therefore devised a checklist of points to help her reach a decision. She also decided that any learner who achieves a lower mark will not be referred, but will be given the opportunity to respond verbally to the questions.

In this example, Haedish has made a decision to differentiate for her learners. However, she must first check with the other staff that this is acceptable and, if so, they must also be able to offer the same option to their learners. This will ensure that all assessors are being fair to all learners. She should also share her checklist with the other staff to ensure that they are all being fair when making decisions.

If you are writing multiple-choice questions, there should be a clear question and three or four possible answers. The question is known as the *stem*, the answer is called the *key*, and the wrong answers are called *distracters*. Answers and distracters should always be similar in length and complexity (or words, diagrams and pictures). They should not be confusing, and there should only be one definite key.

Good example of a multiple-choice question

Formative assessment is always:

(A) before the programme commences

(B) at the beginning of the programme

(C) ongoing throughout the programme

(D) when the programme ends

You will see that all the answers contain a similar amount and type of words. The term *programme* is used in all responses for consistency. None of the answers contains a clue from the question. A, B and D are the distracters and C is the correct answer (the key).

Poor example of the same multiple-choice question

Formative assessment is always:

(A) carried out when the learners are interviewed on a one-to-one basis before the course starts

(b) at the beginning

(C) ongoing throughout the programme

(d) when the qualification ends and all assessments have taken place

You will see that each answer has a different amount and type of words, uses both capital and lower case letters for the question numbers, and *course*, *programme* and *qualification* are used to denote the same term. A, b and d are the distracters and C is the correct answer (the key).

If you are using multiple-choice tests with learners, it might be an idea to give them a few examples to practise with first. This is just in case they are not familiar with the format. It can also be beneficial for learners to write a few multiple-choice questions themselves to test the rest of the group. This gives them an insight into how the questions are formatted and how thoroughly they need to read exactly what the question is asking, before choosing a response.

If you are using the same questions with different learners at different times, be careful in case they give the answers to each other. You may need to rephrase some questions if your learners are struggling with an answer as poor answers are often the result of poor questions. For essay and short-answer tests you should create sample answers, to have something with which to compare. If there are several assessors involved, you could all answer the questions and then compare the responses to each other. This will help ensure the questions have been interpreted correctly, aid the standardisation process and give consistent marks to learners. Be careful with the use of jargon – just because you understand it doesn't mean your learners will. You might want to grade the responses once all your learners' work has been submitted. Otherwise, if you assess the first one in, you have nothing to compare it to and might feel it's really good and therefore give it a high grade. However, when the others are submitted they might be better and it could be too late to amend the first one's grade.

If you issue any assessment activities as homework, you need to plan your own time accordingly to ensure you are able to assess all the work that will be submitted by a certain date. It could be that your organisation expects you to assess and give feedback within a certain time period, for example seven days.

Extension Activity

Write a few questions based on your subject in different formats, such as open, closed, probing or multiple-choice. Try them out with your learners and evaluate which were the best to use and why.

Minimising risks

Assessing a learner and confirming their success can be very rewarding. However, there are risks involved and being aware of these will hopefully help to avoid them. This is particularly the case with summative assessment, which is to confirm achievement. However, there can still be risks with formative assessment, which is to check on progress. The risks apply not only with regard to the health, safety and welfare of all concerned, but what might occur in your own area of responsibility for your particular subject. Just ask yourself what could possibly go wrong, and if you can think of something, then there is a risk. A bullet-point summary of risks is included on page 83, at the end of this section.

Learner risks

You need to minimise risks such as putting unnecessary stress upon learners, over-assessing, under-assessing, or being unfair and expecting too much too soon. Some learners might not be ready to be observed for a practical skill, or feel so pressured by target dates for a theory test that they resort to colluding or plagiarising work. If learners are under pressure, or have any issues or concerns that have not been addressed, they could be disadvantaged and might decide not to continue with the programme.

Plagiarism and authenticity

When assessing written work, you need to be aware that some learners, intentionally or not, might plagiarise the work of others. Plagiarism is the wrongful use of someone else's work. Authenticity is the rightful and confirmed use of your own work. You need to be aware of learners colluding or plagiarising work, particularly now that so much information is available via the internet. Learners should take responsibility for referencing any sources in all work submitted, and may be required to sign a declaration or an authenticity statement. If you suspect plagiarism, you could type a few of their words into an internet search engine or specialist software and see what appears. You would then have to challenge your learner as to whether it was intentional or not, and follow your organisation's plagiarism procedure.

If assessors and learners are completing and/or submitting documents electronically, there might not be an opportunity to add a real signature to confirm the authenticity of the document. However, many companies are now accepting a scanned signature or an email address, providing the identity of the person has been confirmed.

If you are assessing the work of learners you might not have met in person, for example by e-assessment, it can be very difficult to ensure the authenticity of their work. Your organisation might require each learner to attend an interview at some point and bring along some form of photo identification such as a driving licence, passport or employee card.

Unfortunately, some learners do cheat, copy or plagiarise the work of others. Sometimes this is deliberate; at other times it is due to a lack of knowledge of exactly what was required, or a misunderstanding when referencing quotes within work. If you feel the work that has been submitted to you might not be the actual work of your learner, ask them some questions about it. This will confirm their knowledge, or otherwise. If you feel it isn't their work, you will need to confront them and let them know you will take the matter further. At this point your learner may confess, or they may have what they consider a legitimate excuse. However, you must be certain the work is their own, otherwise it could be classed as fraud.

Example

Gary was marking assignments from his ICT Functional Skills learners and noticed that two of them had an identical paragraph in them. He typed a few of the words from the paragraph into a search engine. He found that they were from an assignment which a previous learner had uploaded to a study skills website. He challenged his learners, who said they had left their work until quite late to hand in, and hadn't realised they couldn't copy and paste text. Gary reminded them about the Acceptable Use of ICT Code of Practice and said that anything they used which belonged to someone else must be correctly referenced. He then gave them another assignment to complete and discussed the importance of managing their time to meet deadlines.

It is easier to compare the work of your own learners as you are familiar with them; however, other assessors in your organisation might also assess the same programme with different learners. In this case, the internal quality assurer may pick up on issues when they are sampling learner work. It is difficult to check and compare the work of all learners, therefore the importance of authenticity must be stressed to everyone at the commencement of their programme and continually throughout. Asking learners to sign and date hard copies of work, or adding a statement to electronic work is a useful way of getting them to accept responsibility.

Some ways of checking the authenticity of learners' work include:

- Spelling, grammar and punctuation – you know your learner speaks in a certain way at a certain level, yet their written work does not reflect this.

- Work that includes quotes which have not been referenced – without a reference source, this is direct plagiarism and could be a breach of copyright.

- Word-processed work that contains different fonts and sizes of text – this shows it could have been copied from the internet, or someone else's electronic file.

- Handwritten work that looks different from your learner's normal handwriting, or is not the same style or language as normally used, or word-processed work when they would normally write by hand.

- Work that refers to information you haven't taught, or is not relevant.

Electronic assessment systems often allow contact to take place between the learner and assessor through a website platform. You could communicate in this way, or via email, and then compare the style of writing in the submitted work to that within the communications.

The Copyright, Designs and Patents Act (1988) is the current UK copyright law. Copying the work of others without their permission would infringe the Act. Copyright is where an individual or organisation creates something as an original, and has the right to control the ways in which their work may be used by others. Normally the person who created the work will own the exclusive rights. However, if the work is produced as part of your employment, for example, if you created several handouts or a workbook for your learners, then normally the work will belong to your organisation. Learners may be in breach of this Act if they plagiarise or copy the work of others without making reference to the original author.

Assessor risks

There are risks on your part as an assessor; for example, there may be pressure to pass learners quickly due to funding and targets, which might lead you to pass something that you normally wouldn't. There is also the risk that you might unknowingly offer favouritism or bias towards some learners over others.

A risk to yourself could be if you carry out assessments in the work environment and visit places with which you are not familiar. You might need to travel early or late in the dark, find locations on foot, take public transport, or drive to areas you are not familiar with. If you are visiting places on your own, you will be classed as a lone worker and your organisation should have a policy for your protection. Having a mobile phone is helpful in such situations; if not, note where the nearest public phone is should you need it. You may find it useful to search the internet for the postcode you are visiting. This will give you a street map and pictures of the local area to enable you to visualise where you are going beforehand.

The type of employment contract you have might pose a risk. For example, you might be part time and work for more than one organisation, or be working for an agency or for yourself on a freelance basis. If you don't have a permanent contract, it could be difficult to determine who you report to if you have any concerns. If you are assessing towards a qualification, you will need to know who your internal quality assurer is, as they should support you in your role. Standardisation of practice might be difficult if assessors are not all in the same location or working for the same organisation.

You might not have access to the resources that permanent members of staff have and may need to provide your own, such as personal protective equipment (PPE). There's also the risk of pressure upon you if your learners are allocated to you on a case-load basis. For example, you might only be paid if your allocated number of learners complete the qualification.

Other risks

If you are assessing in the work environment, you might come across employers who are not supportive of their staff and may put barriers in their way. For example, someone might make it difficult for you to visit at a certain time to carry out a formal assessment. Careful planning and communication with everyone concerned will be necessary.

It could be that if you have close friends or relatives among those you are required to assess, you might not be allowed to do so, or, if you do, your decisions would need to be countersigned by another impartial assessor. Your decisions should also go through an internal quality assurance process. If it's an accredited qualification, the awarding organisation will be able to give you guidance regarding this.

If you have any concerns regarding risks to yourself, your learners, or your assessment decisions, you must discuss them with someone, such as your supervisor or internal quality assurer. Being aware of any risks to the assessment process, yourself or your learners, and taking opportunities to discuss any issues should help minimise their occurrence.

Activity

Locate and access your organisation's codes of practice, such as:

- *acceptable use of ICT*

- *code of conduct*

- *duty of care*

- *lone working*

- *plagiarism and authenticity.*

Have a look at them and see how they can help you and your learners to stay safe. Safe in this context relates to both health and safety, and whether the assessment methods are sufficiently robust to make a reliable decision.

Situations which could pose a risk to assessment include the following (in alphabetical order):

- a lack of confidence by the assessor to make correct decisions

- a lack of standardisation activities leading to one assessor giving more of an advantage to a learner than another assessor of the same subject

- a learner copying another learner's work

- a learner's lack of confidence or resistance to being assessed

- an assessor not taking into account a learner's particular needs

- an unsuitable environment for assessment to take place

- answers to questions being obtained inappropriately by learners which leads to cheating

- assessing relatives without having decisions countersigned

- assessing written work too quickly and not noticing errors, plagiarism or cheating

- assessors giving learners the answers or doing some of the work for them

- assessors using inappropriate assessment activities

- assessors using leading questions to obtain the correct answers they require

- assessors visiting unfamiliar places and under pressure to arrive by a certain time

- awarding organisations prescribing assessment methods which might not complement the qualification, a learner's needs or the learning environment

- changes to qualifications or standards not being interpreted correctly by assessors, or not being communicated to assessors by others

- employers not supportive of assessment in the workplace, or are not good at communicating with the assessor

- favouritism and bias by an assessor towards some learners over others

- feedback to the learner which is unhelpful or ineffective

- high turnover of staff, resulting in inconsistent support to learners

- ineffective internal quality assurance system

- instructions too complex or too easy for the learners' ability

- insufficient or incorrect action/assessment planning

- internal and external quality assurance action points not being correctly communicated to those concerned, or not carried out

- lack of resources or time to perform the assessment role correctly

- learners creating a portfolio of evidence which is based on quantity rather than quality, i.e. submitting too much evidence which does not meet the requirements

- learners not registered with an awarding organisation prior to being assessed for a qualification

- learners submitting the work of others as their own

- learners using quotes from others when answering theory questions and not referencing them, leading to plagiarism

- marking and grading carried out incorrectly by assessors

- misinterpreting the assessment requirements and/or criteria (by learners and assessors)

- pressure on assessors to pass learners quickly due to funding and targets

- time pressures and targets put upon learners

- unreliable witness testimonies from the workplace

- unsuitable assessment methods, i.e. an observation when questions would suffice

- unsuitable assessment types, i.e. summative being used instead of formative

- unwelcome disruptions and interruptions when assessing, such as noise or telephone calls.

Extension Activity

What risks do you feel you will encounter when assessing learners, and how will you overcome them? Have you ever been placed in a difficult situation that could cause a risk to yourself or to your learners? If so, what would you do differently next time?

Table 3.3 Methods of assessment, approaches and activities, with their strengths and limitations

Method/ approach/ activity	Description	Strengths	Limitations
Activities – group or individual	Different tasks carried out by learners to demonstrate their skills, knowledge, understanding and/or attitudes.	Can be individual, paired or group tasks. Ideal as a formative assessment approach to establish progress at a given point during a session, or as a summative approach for workplace tasks.	If paired or grouped, assessor must establish achievement of individuals. Can be time-consuming for the assessor to devise and facilitate.
Assignments	Can be practical or theoretical tasks which can assess various aspects of a subject or qualification over a period of time.	Consolidates learning. Several aspects of a qualification can be assessed. Some assignments are set by the awarding organisation who will give clear marking criteria. Learners might be able to add to their work if they don't meet all the requirements first time.	Everything must have been taught beforehand or be known by the learner. Questions can be misinterpreted. Can be time-consuming for learners to complete. Must be individually assessed and written feedback given. Assessor might be biased when marking.
Blended assessments	Using more than one method of assessment, usually including technology.	Several methods of assessment can be combined, enabling all learning preferences to be reached.	Not all learners may have access to the technology.
Buzz groups	Short topics to be discussed in small groups.	Allows learner interaction and focuses ideas. Checks understanding. Doesn't require formal feedback.	Learners may digress. Specific points could be lost. Checking individual learning may be difficult.
Case studies/ scenarios	Can be a hypothetical situation, a description of an actual event or an incomplete event, enabling learners to explore the situation.	Can make topics more realistic, enhancing motivation and interest. Can be carried out individually or in a group situation. Builds on current knowledge and experience.	If carried out as a group activity, roles should be defined and individual contributions assessed. Time should be allowed for a debrief. Must have clear outcomes. Can be time-consuming to prepare and assess.

(Continued)

85

Table 3.3 (Continued)

Method/approach/activity	Description	Strengths	Limitations
Checklists	A list of criteria which must be met to confirm competence or achievement.	Can form part of an ongoing record of achievement or job profile. Assessment can take place when a learner is ready. Ensures all criteria are documented.	Learners may lose their copy and not remember the details of what they have achieved. Assessors might be tempted to 'tick all the boxes' when a learner hasn't fully met everything.
Discussions with learners, also known as professional discussions	A one-to-one conversation between the assessor and learner based around the assessment criteria.	Ideal way to assess aspects which are more difficult to observe, are rare occurrences, or take place in restricted or confidential settings. Useful to support observations to check knowledge. Learners can describe how they carry out various activities. Develops communication skills. Useful for visual or kinaesthetic learners who might struggle with written work.	A record must be kept of the discussion, e.g. audio/digital/visual along with notes. Needs careful planning as it is a discussion not a question-and-answer session. Learners need time to prepare. Assessor needs to be experienced at using open and probing questions, and listening carefully to the responses to ensure they have met the requirements.
Discussions/debates	Learners talk about a relevant topic either in groups or pairs.	Allows freedom to express different viewpoints. Promotes questions and discussions. Can contribute to meeting assessment criteria.	Easy to digress. Assessor needs to keep the group focused and set a time limit. Some learners may not get involved, while others may dominate. Assessor needs to manage the contributions of each individual and know what has been achieved and by whom. Can be time-consuming. Learners may need to research a topic in advance. Can lead to arguments.

Method/ approach/ activity	Description	Strengths	Limitations
E-assessments/ online assessments	*Electronic assessment* – assessment using information and communication technology (ICT). *Synchronous* – assessor and learner are simultaneously present, communicating in real time. *Asynchronous* – assessor and learner are interacting at different times.	Teaching, learning and assessment can take place in a virtual learning environment (VLE). Assessment can take place at a time to suit learners. Participation is widened. Results and feedback can be instantly generated. Less paperwork for the assessor. Improves computer skills. Can be blended with other assessment methods. Groups, blogs, forums and chat rooms can be set up to improve communication.	Learners need access to a computer or suitable device and need to be computer literate. Reliable internet connection needed. Self-discipline is needed. Clear targets must be set. Authenticity of learner's work may need validating. Technical support may be required.
Essays	A formal piece of written text, produced by a learner, for a specific topic.	Useful for academic subjects. Can check a learner's English skills at specific levels. Enhances a learner's knowledge by using research and reading.	Not suitable for lower-level learners. Marking can be time-consuming. Plagiarism can be an issue. Doesn't usually have a right or wrong answer, therefore difficult to mark. Learners need good writing skills.
Examinations	A formal activity which must be carried out in certain conditions.	Can be *open book*, or *open notes*, enabling learners to have books and notes with them. Some learners like the challenge of a formal examination and cope well. Examinations are often perceived to have greater rigour than some other assessment methods.	Invigilation required. Security arrangements to be in place prior to and afterwards for examination papers. Learners may have been taught purely to pass expected questions by using past papers, therefore they may forget everything afterwards. Some learners may be anxious.

(Continued)

Table 3.3 (Continued)

Method/ approach/ activity	Description	Strengths	Limitations
Examinations (continued)		Can be externally created and assessed by an awarding organisation, saving the assessor time. If externally created but internally assessed, the awarding organisation should provide sample answers, making marking more consistent and less time-consuming.	Can be *closed book*, or *closed notes*, not allowing learners to have books and notes with them. Results might take a while to be marked and processed if external. If a learner fails, they may have to wait a period of time before a retake.
Group work	Enables learners to carry out a specific activity, for example, problem-solving. Can be practical or theoretical.	Allows interaction between learners. Encourages participation and variety. Rotating group members enables all learners to work with each other. Helps learners evaluate their performance and other skills, such as team-work, leadership, communication and life skills.	Careful management by the assessor is required regarding time limits, progress, and ensuring all group members are clear about the requirements. Could be personality problems or conflict in different ways of working between team members. One person may dominate. Difficult to assess individual contributions. Time is needed for a thorough debrief.
Holistic assessment	Enables learners to demonstrate several aspects of a programme or qualification at the same time.	Similar criteria from different units can be assessed at the same time. Makes evidence collection and demonstration of achievement and competence much more efficient. Can incorporate a range of assessment methods. Helps learners link knowledge to practice.	Could confuse the learner if aspects are assessed which were not planned for.
Homework	Activities carried out between sessions, e.g. answering questions to check knowledge.	Learners can complete work at a time and place that suits them. Maintains interest between sessions. Encourages learners to stretch themselves further. Consolidates learning so far.	Clear targets and time limits must be set. Learners might not do it, or get someone else to do it for them. Must be marked/assessed and individual feedback given.

Method/approach/activity	Description	Strengths	Limitations
Interviews	A one-to-one discussion, usually before a programme commences, or partway through to discuss progress.	Enables the assessor to determine how much a learner knows. Enables the assessor to get to know each learner, and discuss any issues.	Not all learners may react well when interviewed. Needs careful planning, and consistency of questions between learners. Detailed records need to be kept.
Learner statements	Learners write how they have met the assessment criteria.	Enables learners to take ownership of their achievements.	Learners might misinterpret the assessment criteria and/or write too much or too little. Another assessment method should be used in addition to confirm practical skills.
Learning journal/diary or reflective account	Learners keep a record of their progress, their reflections and thoughts, and reference these to the assessment criteria.	Helps assess English skills. Useful for higher-level programmes. Journal can be paper-based, electronic, audio or video-based to suit the learner and their programme.	Should be specific to the learning taking place and be analytical rather than descriptive. Content needs to remain confidential. Can be time-consuming and/or difficult to read/watch or hear.
Observations	Watching learners perform a skill and/or demonstrate a change in knowledge or behaviour.	Enables skills to be seen in action. Learners can make a mistake (if it is safe) enabling them to realise their areas for development. Learners can be observed again if they didn't fully achieve the requirements. Can be used as a starting point to generate the content for a professional discussion or question-and-answer session. Can assess several aspects at the same time (holistic assessment). Ensures authenticity (providing the assessor knows the learner).	Timing must be arranged to suit each learner. Communication needs to take place with others (if applicable). No permanent record unless visually recorded. Questions must be asked to confirm knowledge and understanding (either during or after the observation depending on the task, i.e. if the learner is in the workplace with customers, it would be intrusive and inappropriate for the assessor to interrupt). Assessor might not be objective with decision. Learner might put on an act for the assessor which isn't how they normally perform (could be better or worse).

(Continued)

Table 3.3 (Continued)

Method/approach/activity	Description	Strengths	Limitations
Peer assessment	Learners give feedback to their peers after an activity.	Promotes learner and peer interaction, involvement and team-work. Learners may accept comments from peers better than those from the assessor. Enables learners to assess each other. Activities can often correct misunderstandings and consolidate learning without intervention by the assessor.	Everyone needs to understand the assessment criteria and requirements. Needs to be carefully managed to ensure no personality conflicts or unjustified comments. Assessor needs to confirm progress and achievements, which might differ. Some peers may be anxious about giving feedback, perhaps if their peer had not done well. Should be supported with other assessment methods. Needs careful management and training in how to give feedback.
Portfolios of evidence	A formal record of evidence (manual or electronic) produced by learners to meet performance or qualification requirements.	Ideal for learners who don't like formal tests and exams. The assessor can involve the learner to negotiate their action plan and further assessment. Can be compiled over a period of time to reflect ongoing performance and knowledge. Learner centred, therefore promotes autonomy and ongoing reflection. Evidence can be left in its natural location to be viewed by the assessor.	Authenticity and currency to be checked. Computer access required to assess electronic portfolios. Tendency for learners to produce a large quantity of evidence. All evidence must be cross-referenced to the relevant criteria. Can be time-consuming to assess. Confidentiality of documents within the portfolio must be maintained.
Practical activities/tasks	Assesses a learner's skills in action.	Actively involves learners. Can meet all learning preferences if carefully set. Can be designed and contextualised to be relevant and interesting for learners.	Some learners may not respond well to practical activities or have an 'off day' when performing. Can be time-consuming to create. Questions must be asked to ascertain knowledge and understanding.

Method/ approach/ activity	Description	Strengths	Limitations
Presentations	Learners deliver a topic, often using information and communication technology.	Can be individual or in a group. Can assess skills, knowledge, understanding, behaviour and attitudes. Develops presentation skills and equips learners with skills for the workplace, such as communication.	If a group presentation, individual contributions must be assessed. Some learners may be nervous or anxious in front of others.
Products (reviewing learner evidence and portfolios)	Evidence produced by a learner to prove competence, e.g. paintings, models, video, audio, photos, documents.	Assessor can see what the learner has done, along with the final product. Learners feel a sense of achievement, e.g. by displaying their work in an exhibition or producing a portfolio of paper-based or electronic evidence.	Authenticity needs to be checked if the assessor has not been seen the learner producing the work. Learners might forget to document and evaluate the process, losing opportunities for the submission of further evidence.
Professional discussions (see *Discussions with learners*)			
Projects	A longer-term activity enabling learners to provide evidence which meets the assessment criteria.	Can be interesting and motivating. Can be individual or group led. Can meet all learning preferences. Encourages research and creativity skills. Learners could choose their own topics and devise tasks.	Clear outcomes must be set, along with a time limit; they must be relevant, realistic and achievable. Progress should be checked regularly. If a group is carrying out the project, ensure that each individual's input is assessed. Learners with poor team-working skills might miss sessions or not engage with their team, which might lead the assessor to set an additional, individual project to ensure the learner generates the required evidence. Assessor might be biased when marking.

(Continued)

Table 3.3 (Continued)

Method/ approach/ activity	Description	Strengths	Limitations
Puzzles, quizzes, word searches, crosswords, etc.	A fun way of assessing learning in an informal way.	Fun activities to test skills, knowledge and/or understanding. Useful back-up activity if learners finish earlier than planned. Useful way to assess progress of lower-level learners. Good for assessing retention of facts.	Can seem trivial to mature learners. Does not assess a learner's level of understanding or ability to apply their knowledge to situations. Can be time-consuming to create and assess.
Questions	A key technique for assessing understanding and stimulating thinking; can be informal or formal, written or verbal. Questions can be closed, hypothetical, leading, open, probing, multiple-choice.	Can be short answer or long essay style. Can challenge and promote a learner's potential. A question bank can be devised which could be used again for different learners. Can test critical arguments or thinking and reasoning skills. Oral questions suit some learners more than others, e.g. a learner who has dyslexia might prefer to talk through their responses.	Closed questions only give a 'yes' or 'no' response, which doesn't demonstrate knowledge or understanding. Questions must be written carefully, i.e. be unambiguous, and can be time-consuming to prepare. If the same questions are used with other learners, they could share their answers. Written responses might be the work of others, e.g. copied or plagiarised. Expected responses or grading criteria need to be produced beforehand to ensure consistency and validity of marking. May need to rephrase some questions if learners are struggling with an answer.
Recognition of prior learning (RPL)	Assessing what has previously been learnt, experienced and achieved to find a suitable starting point for further assessments.	Ideal for learners who have achieved aspects of the programme prior to commencement. No need for learners to duplicate work, or be reassessed. Values previous learning, experiences and achievements.	Checking the authenticity and currency of the evidence provided is crucial. Previous learning, experiences and achievements might not be relevant in relation to current requirements. Can be time-consuming for both learner to prove, and the assessor to assess.

Method/ approach/ activity	Description	Strengths	Limitations
Reflective account	Learners reflect upon how they have put theory into practice and link this to the criteria being assessed.	A type of self-assessment. Can be formally assessed, therefore can count towards achievement as well as progress. Useful for higher-level learners. Learners can include photos to illustrate their points and provide further evidence and links to work saved online or on social media.	Can be time-consuming to assess. Learners need the skills of reflective writing and cross-referencing. Learners might feel they have achieved more than they have.
Reports, research and dissertations	Learners produce a document to inform, recommend and/or make suggestions based on the assessment criteria.	Useful for higher-level learners. Promotes critical and analytical skills. Encourages the use of research techniques.	Learners need research and academic writing skills. Can be time-consuming to assess. Plagiarism and authenticity can be an issue.
Role-plays	Learners act out a hypothetical situation.	Enables the assessor to observe learners' behaviour. Encourages participation. Can lead to debates. Links theory to practice.	Can be time-consuming. Clear roles must be defined. Not all learners may want or be able to participate. Some learners may get too dramatic. Individual contributions must be assessed. Time needed for a thorough debrief.
Self-assessment	Learners decide how they have met the assessment criteria, or how they are progressing at a given time.	Promotes learner involvement and personal autonomy. Encourages learners to check their own work. Encourages reflection.	Learners may feel they are doing better or worse than they actually are. Assessor needs to discuss progress and achievements with each learner to confirm their decisions. Learners need to be specific about what they have achieved and what they need to do to complete any gaps. Difficult for the learner to be objective when making a decision.

(Continued)

Table 3.3 (Continued)

Method/ approach/ activity	Description	Strengths	Limitations
Skills tests	Designed to find out the level of skill or previous experience/knowledge towards a particular subject or vocation.	Could be online or computer based to enable a quick assessment, e.g. in maths. Results can be used as starting point for learning or progression.	Learners might be apprehensive of formal tests. Feedback might not be immediate. If electronically generated, feedback might not be useful or developmental.
Simulation	Imitation or acting out of an event or situation.	Useful when it is not possible to carry out a task for real: e.g. to assess whether or not learners can successfully evacuate a building in the event of a fire.	Only enables an assessment of a hypothetical situation; learners may act very differently in a real situation. Not usually accepted as demonstration of competence.
Team-building exercises/ energisers	A fun and light-hearted way of re-energising learners. Can be used to informally assess skills, knowledge and attitudes.	A good way of learners getting to work with each other. Can revitalise a flagging session.	Not all learners may want, or be able, to take part. Some learners may think they are insignificant and time-wasting. Careful explanations are needed to link the experience to the topic being assessed.
Tests (and multiple-choice tests)	A formal assessment situation.	Cost-effective method, as the same test can be used with large numbers of learners. Some test responses can be scanned into a computer for marking and analysis. Other tests can be taken at a computer or online which give immediate results. Questions can be randomly generated to prevent different learners taking the same test.	Needs to be carried out in supervised conditions or via a secure website. Time limits usually required. Can be stressful to learners. Does not take into account any formative progress. Feedback might not be immediate if assessed manually or externally.

Method/ approach/ activity	Description	Strengths	Limitations
Tests (continued)			Learners in other groups might find out the content of the tests from others. Identity of learners needs confirming. Electronic feedback from multiple-choice tests might not be developmental enough to help the learner improve in certain areas.
Tutorials	A one-to-one or group discussion between the assessor and learner, with an agreed purpose, e.g. discussing progress so far.	A good way of informally assessing a learner's progress and/or giving feedback. An opportunity for learners to discuss issues or for informal tuition to take place.	Needs to be in a comfortable, safe and quiet environment, as confidential issues may be discussed. Time may overrun. Records should be maintained and action points followed up.
Video/audio	Recorded evidence of actual achievements.	Direct proof of what was achieved by a learner, i.e. eliminates issues of proving authenticity. Can be reviewed by the assessor and internal quality assurer after the event. Digital facilities are more easily accessible, e.g. using different devices and smart phones.	Can prove expensive to purchase equipment and storage media. Can be time-consuming to set up and use. Technical support may be required. Storage facilities are required. If recorded in the workplace, confidentiality of content may need to be discussed with the employer and a declaration signed. Large files might exceed the maximum upload size for an e-portfolio.

(Continued)

Table 3.3 (Continued)

Method/ approach/ activity	Description	Strengths	Limitations
Walk and talk	A spoken and visual way of assessing a learner's competence.	Enables a learner to 'walk and talk' through their product evidence within their work environment. Gives an audit trail of the evidence relating to the assessment criteria. Saves time producing a full portfolio of evidence; can be recorded as evidence of the discussion. Useful where sensitive and confidential information is dealt with.	Can be time-consuming. Can be difficult for the assessor to appreciate all the evidence. Difficult for quality assurers to sample the evidence.
Witness testimonies	A statement from a person who is familiar with the learner (they could also be an expert in the standards being assessed and the occupation of the learner in the work environment).	The witness can confirm competence or achievements for situations which might not regularly occur, or include confidential and security aspects. The witness spends more time with the learner and could observe aspects which are more difficult to plan for, e.g. dealing with a difficult customer or an emergency situation. Witness testimonies can be recoded in written or audio/visual format.	The assessor must confirm the suitability of the witness and check the authenticity of any statements. Learners could write the statement and the witness might sign it while not understanding the content.
Worksheets and gapped handouts	Interactive handouts to check knowledge (can also be electronic). Blank spaces can be used for learners to fill in the missing words.	Informal assessment activity which can be done individually, in pairs or groups. Useful for lower-level learners. Can be created at different degrees of difficulty to address differentiation.	Mature learners may consider them inappropriate. Too many worksheets can be boring. Learners might not be challenged enough.

Summary

Understanding the different assessment methods and activities you could use with your learners will help make the process interesting, stimulating and motivating. Being aware of the risks to assessment will hopefully make you thoughtful and cautious when planning which methods to use.

You might like to carry out further research by accessing the books and websites listed at the end of this chapter.

This chapter has covered the following topics:

- Methods of assessment
- The role of technology in assessment
- Questioning techniques
- Minimising risks

References and further information

Boud, D. (1995) *Enhancing Learning Through Self-assessment*. London: Kogan Page.

Cabinet Office (2014) *Government Digital Inclusion Strategy*. Available at: www.gov.uk/government/publications/government-digital-inclusion-strategy/government-digital-inclusion-strategy.

Craft, A. (2011) *Creativity and Educational Futures: Learning in a Digital Age*. Stoke on Trent: Trentham Books.

Gravells, A. (2014) *Achieving your Assessment and Quality Assurance Units (TAQA)*. London: Learning Matters/SAGE.

Gravells, A. (2014) *The Award in Education and Training* (revised edn). London: Learning Matters/SAGE.

Gravells, A. and Simpson, S. (2014) *The Certificate in Education and Training*. London: Learning Matters/SAGE.

Hill, C. (2008) *Teaching with E-learning in the Lifelong Learning Sector* (2nd edn). Exeter: Learning Matters.

JISC (2010) *Effective Assessment in a Digital Age: A Guide to Technology-enhanced Assessment and Feedback*. Bristol: JISC Innovation Group. Available at: www. jisc.ac.uk/digiassess.

Koc, S. and Xiongyi Liu (2015) *Assessment in Online and Blended Learning Environments*. Charlotte: Information Age Publishing.

Kolb, D. A. (1984) *Experiential Learning: Experience as the Source for Learning and Development*. New Jersey: Prentice-Hall.

Ofqual (2009) *Authenticity – A Guide for Teachers*. Coventry: Ofqual.

Pachler, N. et al. (2009) *Scoping a Vision for Formative E-assessment (FEASST)*. Bristol: JISC.

Parr, C. (2013) 'FE colleges "may lose students to Moocs"', in *Times Higher Education*, 9 May. Available at: www.timeshighereducation.co.uk/news/fe-colleges-may-lose-students-to-moocs/2003709.article

Poore, M. (2013) *Using Social Media in the Classroom: A Best Practice Guide*. London: SAGE.

Read, H. (2011) *The Best Assessor's Guide*. Bideford: Read On Publications.

Read, H. and Gravells, A. (2015) *The Best Vocational Trainer's Guide*. Bideford: Read On Publications.

Starkey, L. (2012) *Teaching and Learning in the Digital Age*. Abingdon: Routledge.

Tummons, J. (2011) *Assessing Learning in the Lifelong Learning Sector* (3rd edn). Exeter: Learning Matters.

White, J. (2015) *Digital Literacy Skills for FE Teachers*. London: SAGE.

Wilson, L.A. (2012) *Practical Teaching: A Guide to Assessment and Quality Assurance*. Andover: Cengage Learning.

Websites

Assistive technology – **www.washington.edu/doit/assistive-technology**

Dropbox file sharing – **www.dropbox.com**

FELTAG Report (2014) *Paths Forward to a Digital Future for Further Education and Skills* – **http://feltag. org.uk/**

Initial assessments for ICT – **www.tes.co.uk/teaching-resource/ict-initial-assessments-6177727**

JISC (Joint Information Systems Committee) – **www.jisc.ac.uk**

JISC: Using digital media in new learning models (flipped and blended learning) – **http://tinyurl. com/nl62z4k**

Online course design – **www.theedadvocate.org/seven-deadly-sins-of-online-course-design/?doing_wp_cron=1435573701.17410802841186523437 50**

Online free courses in various subjects – **www.vision2learn.net**

Online games – **www.npted.org/schools/sandfieldsComp/games/Pages/Game-Downloads.aspx**

Online presentations – **www.prezi.com**

Open Office computer software – **www.openoffice.org/download/**

Peer assessment and self-assessment – **www.nclrc.org/essentials/assessing/peereval.htm**

Pinterest – **https://uk.pinterest.com**

Plagiarism – **www.plagiarism.org** and **www.plagiarismadvice.org**

Puzzle software –

www.about.com www.crossword-compiler.com

www.educational-software-directory.net/game/puzzle

http://hotpot.uvic.ca

www.mathsnet.net

Social media –

www.facebook.com

https://instagram.com

www.linkedin.com

https://plus.google.com

www.twitter.com

Teacher training videos for using ICT – **www.teachertrainingvideos.com/latest.html**

Using computers and technology – **http://digitalunite.com/**

Using Microsoft programs – **www.reading.ac.uk/internal/its/training/its-training-index.aspx**

Using VLEs – **www.ofsted.gov.uk/resources/virtual-learning-environments-e-portfolio**

Video email – **http://mailvu.com/**

YouTube – **www.youtube.com**

4 RECORDING PROGRESS AND ACHIEVEMENT

Introduction

Throughout the assessment process, you will need to keep records to provide an audit trail of your learners' progress and achievement, and to satisfy any internal and external requirements. To make a decision as to what your learner has achieved, you need to ensure that all the relevant assessment requirements have been met. This could be towards a qualification, a set of standards, or to confirm competent performance in the workplace. You therefore need to be confident yourself that you understand exactly what you are assessing before you make a decision and give feedback.

This chapter will explore how you can make a valid and reliable decision, give feedback to your learners in a constructive way, and maintain relevant records.

This chapter will cover the following topics:

- Making assessment decisions
- Providing feedback
- Reviewing learner progress
- Record keeping

Making assessment decisions

To know that learning has occurred, some form of assessment must take place, which results in an accurate decision. The decision relates to what has or has not been achieved by your learner. Decisions should be in accordance with the requirements of what has been assessed, and full records must be maintained, usually for at least three years. It is quite a responsibility to confirm an achievement (or otherwise), as it can affect your learner's personal and professional development. Your learner may need to pass certain criteria to achieve a promotion at work, or they may want to achieve a qualification for personal or professional fulfilment.

You must always remain *objective*, i.e. by making a decision based on your learner's competence towards set criteria. You should not be *subjective*, i.e. by making a decision based on your own opinions or other factors such as your learner's personality. However, some qualifications or job roles might require the learner to demonstrate the correct attitude, behaviour and manners. This could be where it's part of their job role and you would then have to make relevant comments. Hopefully, you are experienced as well as knowledgeable regarding what is being assessed, and may have performed the requirements yourself at some time. This will help you see if your learner has performed to an exceptionally high level, i.e. gone above the requirements of what was expected. However, be careful not to compare your learner's performance to your own expectations. If the learner has met the criteria then they have achieved what they were meant to. If they have achieved more, you can comment on this in a positive way and encourage them to continue to excel.

When making a decision, you need to base it on everything you assess. If you are observing a learner's skills, you could follow this up by asking questions to check their knowledge and understanding. Don't be tempted to give them a grade, for example a distinction or a merit (unless this is a requirement); they have either met or not met the requirements. If your learner did not perform according to the requirements, or answered questions incorrectly, then they will need to do it again. It could be that your learner does know the correct response, but your question was vague or ambiguous. You might need to rephrase your instructions or questions, or enable your learner to carry out further training before being reassessed.

Any written/electronic work your learners complete must always be their own, and they may have to show photo identification, sign an authentication statement or complete a declaration form to prove this. If you have several learners all working towards the same outcomes, you will need to ensure that they have not colluded on any formal assessment activities. Otherwise, you might be crediting them with something their peers have done, or even something they have copied from someone else, or from the internet.

Your decisions should always be *valid, authentic, current, sufficient* and *reliable* (VACSR). You will find more information about this in Chapter 1. You should also be fair and ethical when assessing your learners, making a decision and giving feedback.

- **Fair** – the assessment activity was appropriate to all learners at the required level, was inclusive, i.e. available to all, and differentiated for any particular needs. All learners had an equal chance of an accurate assessment decision.

- **Ethical** – the methods used were right and proper for what was assessed and the context of assessment. The learner's welfare, health, safety and security were not compromised.

Example

Sharron has a group of learners taking the Level 1 Office Procedures qualification. They all completed a multiple-choice test at the end of the classroom session. This was a formative assessment activity which Sharron had devised to check their knowledge. When she marked the papers, she realised all the learners had failed questions 2, 3 and 6. She looked back at the questions and realised they were too vague. This assessment was therefore not 'fair' to the learners. As it was a formative assessment, it did not count towards the achievement of the qualification, therefore Sharron was able to tell her learners what had happened. She amended the multiple-choice questions but then used them with a group of learners who were taking an English qualification. This was not 'ethical', as the learners were not familiar with office procedures.

You may find, when assessing, that your learners haven't achieved everything they should have. You need to base your decision on all the information or evidence available to you at the time. If your learner has not met all the requirements, you need to give constructive feedback, discuss any inconsistencies or gaps, and give advice on what they should do next. If your learner disagrees with the assessment process or your decision, they are entitled to follow your organisation's appeals procedure. Don't get too engrossed with your administrative work or form-filling when making a decision, and forget to inform your learner of what they have achieved.

If you are having difficulty making a decision, discuss this with your supervisor or another assessor to obtain a second opinion. You need to be fully confident when making a decision to confirm that what you have assessed does meet the requirements. Never feel pressured to pass a learner who hasn't fully met the requirements, perhaps due to funding deadlines or targets. You are not doing yourself or your learners any favours by saying they have achieved something when they haven't.

You might notice skills your learners have that they can use in other situations. It is useful to point out any such transferable skills to help them realise other contexts in which they could use them. You might also see other aspects demonstrated in addition to those planned. If this is the case, make sure you include them in your decision; inform your learner what else they have achieved, and update your records accordingly.

If you are assessing work from learners who hand it to you for you to assess later, it would be a good idea to have a system of signing it in and out. Your learner will have put a lot of effort into their work, and would like to know that you will take reasonable care with it. When you have made your decision, given feedback and returned their work, you could ask your learner to sign that they have received it back. If your learner loses their work, you will have your original assessment records to prove that assessment has taken place. If you are assessing work which has been emailed to you, or uploaded online for you to access, there will be the facility for you to add electronic comments to it. This will therefore create a record of what was submitted and when, and what comments and feedback were given and when.

Activity

Ask a colleague if you can observe an assessment activity they are due to carry out. Look at their assessment plan and the assessment materials they use. Observe how they communicate with their learner and others, how they reach their decisions, give feedback and complete their records. Seeing how other assessors plan and assess will help you develop your own assessment, decision-making and feedback skills.

Factors which could influence your judgement and decision

When making a judgement or decision regarding your learner's achievement, you must always follow the assessment requirements, as well as your organisation's quality assurance measures. You must remain objective and not let any factors influence your decision if they are not relevant. If you are influenced for any reason, then there is a strong risk your learner will not achieve based on their own merit.

The following are factors to consider when making a decision.

- **Appeals** – if a learner has made an appeal about a decision you or another assessor have made, you should not feel you must pass them for other assessments if they have not met the requirements. Make sure you follow your organisation's procedures and keep records of your decisions.

- **Complaints** – if a learner has made a complaint about a particular assessment method or the way you have treated them, you must remain objective and not take anything personally. You should not let this influence any future decisions; however, you could ask if another assessor could take on this learner if you feel uncomfortable with the situation.

- **Consistency** – are you being fair to all your learners or are you biased towards some learners more than others for any reason?

- **Methods of assessment** – have you used appropriate or alternative methods, for example asking oral questions rather than issuing written questions for a learner who has dyslexia?

- **Plagiarism** – have any learners copied work from others or the internet, or not referenced their research adequately? You could type a sentence of their work into a search engine to see if it already exists elsewhere.

- **Pressure** – do you feel under pressure to pass learners who are borderline, perhaps due to funding measures, targets, inspectors or employer expectations?

- **Risk assessments** – are any of your learners likely to leave, or do they need extra support for any reason? Don't feel obliged to give too much support, to the extent that your work becomes your learner's.

- **The assessment requirements** – have both you and your learner interpreted these in the same way? Was the activity too easy or too hard?

- **Trends** – is there a pattern, i.e. are most learners making the same mistakes? If so, it could be that they have misinterpreted something, or you have misinformed them or been vague or ambiguous. If this is the case, you could summarise the trends and discuss them with other assessors to standardise practice.

- **Type of assessment** (i.e. formal or informal) – you might be more lenient with informal assessments to encourage progress. However, you do need to be fair and ethical with all your assessment methods and decisions.

- **VACSR** – is your learner's evidence valid, authentic, current, sufficient and reliable? How can you ensure their work meets all these aspects? If you are assessing group work, how do you know what each individual has contributed? If you don't know, you might be attributing achievement to those who haven't contributed much.

If you are in any doubt, you must talk to someone else who is a specialist in your subject area, such as another assessor. Samples of your decisions should be checked via the quality assurance process to ensure that you are assessing correctly, consistently, fairly and ethically. However, this usually takes place after you have made a decision and it might be too late if you have made a positive judgement. You will then need to explain to your learner that they have not passed and that they need to do further work. They might not take this very well.

If you are assessing an accredited qualification, an external quality assurer from the awarding organisation for your subject may also sample your decisions along with your learner's work. You will need to ensure that they have been registered with the appropriate awarding organisation first. It might not be your responsibility to carry out this task, but you should communicate the details of your learners to the relevant staff. You should then receive a list of learners' registration numbers to confirm this.

Ensuring you choose the right method of assessment to carry out with your learners, and making a decision which is fair and ethical will help support your learners towards their achievement.

Extension Activity

Consider what could influence you when making an assessment decision. For example, are the assessment requirements explicit, enabling you to be totally objective, or could they be misinterpreted, making it difficult for you to make a judgement? What would you do if you felt under pressure to pass a learner who had not met all the criteria?

Providing feedback

All learners need to know how they are progressing and what they have achieved so far. Feedback from you will help encourage, motivate and develop them further. It should aim to improve and have an impact upon learning by identifying any additional requirements and areas for progression.

Feedback can be given informally, for example during a discussion, or formally after an assessment activity. Feedback can be verbal or written depending upon the type of assessment you have carried out. If you are with your learners, perhaps observing an activity, you can give verbal feedback immediately. If you are assessing work which has been handed in for marking, you can give written feedback later. You could make developmental notes on your learner's work or sticky notes, for example, to point out any errors in spelling, grammar, punctuation and sentence construction. Encourage your learners to ask questions or get in touch if they need to clarify any points in your feedback, particularly if you are not giving it in person.

Feedback should be based on facts which relate to what has been assessed, and should not be based purely on your personal opinions. The former is objective, the latter is subjective.

However, you can mix the two if relevant. For example, 'Well done, Hannah, you have met all the criteria and I felt the way you handled the situation was really professional.'

When giving feedback, you should always try to be:

- **constructive** – to help retain your learner's motivation

- **specific** – by being factual and stating exactly what was achieved or not achieved

- **developmental** – by encouraging further learning, e.g. reading and research.

Feedback should be formalised by using an assessment document such as a *feedback and action record*. If you complete these manually, give your learner a copy and keep the original yourself for audit purposes. If the form is electronic, it can be added to over time and it will enable both you and your learner to access it when needed. Table 4.1 opposite gives an example from a workplace observation, while Table 4.2 gives one from a training centre assignment.

The advantages of giving feedback are that it:

- can boost your learner's confidence and motivation

- creates opportunities for clarification, discussion and progression

- emphasises progress rather than failure

- enables your learner to appreciate what they need to do to improve or change their practice

- identifies further learning opportunities or actions required

- informs your learner of what they have achieved.

You need to make sure you are not being ambiguous or vague, i.e. leaving your learner not knowing what they have achieved or what they have to do next. You need to be factual regarding what they have achieved in relation to the assessment criteria, and not just give your opinion. It is important to keep your learners motivated, and what you say can help or hinder their progress and confidence.

Example

All Fatima's learners had passed the required assessment criteria for their first assignment. When assessing these, Fatima just wrote 'Pass', along with 'Good' on each piece of work. Although there were a few spelling and grammatical errors within them all, she did not correct any. She didn't have time to make any comments about how each learner could develop further.

While the learners in the example were probably happy they had achieved a pass, they would not be aware of what they could improve upon, what was good about their work, or that they had made some mistakes. They would therefore continue to make these mistakes, as they would not know any different. It could even be that Fatima didn't notice the

Table 4.1 Example feedback and action record (workplace observation)

<table>
<tr><td colspan="4" align="center">Feedback and action record</td></tr>
<tr><td colspan="2">Learner: Irene Jones</td><td colspan="2">Assessor: Jenny Smith</td></tr>
<tr><td colspan="2">Qualification/unit: Level 1 Certificate in Hospitality & Catering (unit 101)</td><td colspan="2">Date: 6 February</td></tr>
</table>

Aspects assessed	Feedback	Action required	Target date
Unit 101.3 Be able to help maintain a hygienic, safe and secure workplace.	I observed Irene on 6 February at the County Leisure Centre to assess her competence in the workplace. I used the awarding organisation's checklists to ensure all the requirements were met and made additional comments regarding what was seen. Irene successfully performed all the requirements of unit 101 and I am pleased to inform her she has passed. Irene obtained a witness testimony from her supervisor, which confirmed she had successfully covered the criteria over a period of time. See the checklist for more detailed comments.	Irene and I will meet on 6 April to complete an assessment plan for unit 102 and review her progress to date. In the meantime, Irene will read the supporting handouts for unit 102 and put theory into practice at the Leisure Centre.	6 April
Unit 101.4 Know how to maintain a hygienic, safe and secure workplace.	I asked oral questions to check knowledge and have digitally recorded these as evidence of achievement. I held a discussion with Irene based on the knowledge requirements, which was also digitally recorded. This has been saved in the computer file under Irene's name and date.		

Achievements	Learning outcomes	Assessment criteria	
Unit 101	101.3 Be able to help maintain a hygienic, safe and secure workplace. 101.4 Know how to maintain a hygienic, safe and secure workplace.	3.1 – 3.5 4.1 – 4.19	

Table 4.2 Example feedback and action record (training centre assignment)

Feedback and action record				
Learner: Marcia Indira			Assessor: Abbi Cross	
Qualification/unit: Level 2 Business, Administration and Finance			Date: 30 October	
Aspects assessed	**Feedback**		**Action required**	**Target date**
2.1 – Generate a range of ideas for a business enterprise.	I like the ideas you have generated for your business; you have come up with some very original concepts. I feel your idea could become a real business opportunity. Do be careful when you are word-processing your work as you have a few spelling errors, for example, 'where' for 'were' and 'been' for 'being'. If you were putting a proposal together to talk to investors you must ensure it is correct and professional. You could consider looking at various enterprise websites to help with your idea.		No action required	
2.2 – Compare the viability of the business enterprise ideas.	You have looked at the viability of your business by researching what is available elsewhere, and compared your ideas to them. I like the way you have presented this task using graphs and tables. You do seem to have a really good idea that would benefit a lot of people. I would recommend in future you use some colour rather than black and white to make your points stand out.		No action required	
2.3 – Select and develop a business idea.	You selected your idea as proposed in 2.1 and have now followed your ideas through to the development of a business plan. Your plan is very professional-looking and has taken into consideration everything we have discussed during the sessions. I enjoyed watching your presentation to your peers regarding your idea and how it will progress to the investment stage. Peer feedback was positive and your own self-evaluation was fair and objective. You have now successfully achieved learning outcome 2 – well done! We will create a separate action plan for the next learning outcome.		No action required	
Achievements	**Learning outcomes**		**Assessment criteria**	
Unit 1: Business Enterprise	2: Be able to develop a business enterprise idea		2.1 Generate a range of ideas for a business enterprise. 2.2 Compare the viability of the business enterprise ideas. 2.3 Select and develop a business idea.	

mistakes. However, you would not want to demoralise your learners by writing too much regarding their first assessment activity; a combination of written and oral feedback might be better to retain motivation.

If you are writing feedback to be read by learners at a later date, you need to appreciate that how you write it may not be how they read it. It is easy to interpret words or phrases differently from what is intended; therefore, if you can, read the feedback to them at the time of returning their work to allow a two-way discussion to take place. If you don't see your learners regularly, you could email feedback to them. If so, don't get too personal with this; keep to the facts but be as positive as possible to retain their motivation. If you are giving individual verbal feedback, consider when and where you will do this, so as not to embarrass your learner in any way, and to allow enough time for any questions they may have.

Consider your tone of voice when speaking, and take into account both your learner's non-verbal signals and your own body language. You might give feedback to a group regarding an activity; if so, make sure your feedback is specific to the group, and/or each individual's contributions. Your learners will like to know how they are progressing, and what they need to do to improve or develop further. Simple statements such as 'Well done' or 'Good' don't tell your learner what was well done or good about their work, or how they can improve. Using your learner's name makes the feedback more personal, being specific enables your learner to appreciate what they need to do to improve, and smiling while giving feedback can be encouraging.

Example

Rashid visits his learners once a month in their work environment to assess their performance. He also sees them once a fortnight in college to support them with their knowledge. Between these times, he marks their assignments and emails informal feedback to them. A typical email reads:

'Helen, you have passed your assignment. I particularly liked the way you compared and contrasted the two theories. Do be careful when proofreading, as you tend to use "were" instead of "where". I will return your assignment when I next see you, along with more detailed written feedback. Do get in touch if you have any questions.'

This feedback is specific and developmental and will help Rashid's learner to stay motivated until he next sees her. Giving feedback this way is also a good method of keeping in touch if you don't see your learners frequently, and gives your learners the opportunity to communicate with you if necessary. Feedback can lose its impact if you leave it too long, and learners may think you are not interested in their progress if they don't hear from you. Emails and written feedback enable you to maintain records, if required, for audit purposes. When giving feedback face to face, it should be given in a suitable and private environment wherever possible.

Feedback should always be:

- based on facts and not opinions

- clear, genuine and unambiguous

- constructive, specific and developmental

- detailed regarding what was or wasn't achieved, and what needs improving or developing further

- documented – records must be maintained for audit purposes and proof of achievement

- focused on the activity not the person

- helpful and honest.

There could be issues on your part, such as not having enough time to write detailed feedback, not being very good with eye contact when giving verbal feedback, or not being able to turn negative points into constructive points. Giving feedback which is constructive and helpful to your learners will come with practice. If you don't take the time to support your learners with encouraging and positive feedback, you will not be helping them to improve in the long term.

You should always give feedback in a way which will make it clear how your learner has met the requirements, what they have achieved (or not) and what they need to do next.

Example

Marcela is working towards the Level 2 Certificate in Customer Service. She has just been observed by her assessor Geoff, who has also marked her responses to the written questions. Geoff gave her verbal feedback, stating: 'Marcela, you've done really well and passed all the criteria for the observation and written questions. You dealt with the irate customer in a pleasant and calm way. However, I would recommend you use the customer's name a bit more when speaking with them to appear friendly. You've met all the requirements; we can now sign that unit off and plan for the next one.'

In this example, the assessor was constructive, specific and developmental with his feedback; Marcela knew that she had achieved the unit, and what she could do to improve for the future. The use of the word 'however' is much better than the word 'but', which can sound negative. The feedback was also worded at the right level for the learner.

Often, the focus of feedback is likely to be on mistakes rather than strengths. If something positive is stated first, any negative comments are more likely to be listened to and acted upon. Starting with a negative point may discourage your learner from listening to anything else that is said. If possible, start with something positive, then state what could be improved, and finish on a developmental note, as in the previous example. This sandwiches the negative aspect between two positive or helpful aspects. However, negative feedback if given skilfully can help your learner if used in the right way. You will need to find out if your organisation has any specific feedback methods they wish you to use, which will ensure a standardised approach across all assessors to all learners. Whatever method you use to give feedback, it should always be backed up by a written record.

The examples in Table 4.1 and Table 4.2 on pages 105 and 106 are of a completed feedback and action record. They show what was carried out, what action needs to be taken and what has been achieved. A copy should be given to the learner and the original kept by the assessor. The records could be completed manually or electronically. The latter should have an electronic date attached to it, the former could be signed and dated. However, you could use the original assessment plan as in Chapter 2 to add the feedback and achievements, therefore only using one form instead of two. This will depend upon your organisation's requirements.

For qualifications in the workplace it is unlikely that learners will complete units one by one, but that their performance will provide naturally occurring evidence across a range of areas. Remember to be holistic when assessing and map achievements to other areas if they have been met. Make sure your feedback indicates what else your learner has achieved and use this towards action planning for your next assessment. Some criteria might require evidence of competent performance over a period of time, so although the learner has achieved the criteria, further examples of performance might be required to complete in full. It is important that you communicate this to your learner to avoid any confusion.

The role of questioning in feedback

The role of questioning in feedback allows your learner to consider their achievements, for example, before you tell them. A good way to do this is to ask your learner how they feel they have done straight after you have assessed them. This gives them the opportunity to recognise their own mistakes, or reflect on what they could have done differently. You could then build on this through feedback, and discuss what needs to be improved and achieved next.

Having good listening skills will help you engage your learners in a conversation by hearing what they are saying, and responding to any questions or concerns. Giving your learners time to talk will encourage them to inform you of things they might not otherwise have said: for example, if something has had an effect upon their progress. Listening for key words will help you focus upon what is being said, such as: 'I struggled with the last part of the assignment.' The key word is *struggled* and you could therefore ask a question: 'What was it that made you struggle?' This would allow a conversation to then take place, giving you the opportunity to help and support your learner.

When using questioning during feedback:

- Allow enough time for your questions and your learner's responses.
- Ask open questions, i.e. those beginning with *who, what, when, where, why* and *how*.

- Avoid trick or complex questions.

- Be aware of your posture, gestures and body language.

- Be conscious of your dialect, accent, pitch and tone of voice.

- Don't ask more than one question in the same sentence.

- Make sure you don't use closed questions to illicit a yes response; learners may feel that is what you want to hear but it doesn't confirm their understanding.

- Use active listening skills to show you are concentrating on hearing what they have to say.

- Try not to say *erm, yeah, okay, you know,* or *does that make sense?*

- Try not to use a lot of jargon.

- Use eye contact.

- Watch your learners' reactions and body language.

Questioning and feedback should always be adapted to the level of your learners. You won't help your learners if you are using higher-level words or jargon when their level of understanding is lower. You should also be aware of where you give the feedback in case you are interrupted or are in a noisy environment.

Different feedback methods

There are many ways you can give feedback to your learners, including:

- **Descriptive** – describe examples of what was achieved, what could be improved and why. Using this method lets you describe what your learner has done, how they have met the required assessment criteria and what they can do to progress further.

- **Evaluative** – usually just a grade such as 8 out of 10, or a statement such as 'Well done' or 'Good'. This method is not descriptive and does not offer helpful or constructive advice. It does not give learners the opportunity to know what was well done, what was good about it, or how they could improve. It's just an evaluation of achievement which doesn't offer detailed feedback.

- **Constructive** – specific and focused to confirm your learner's achievement or to give developmental points in a positive and helpful way.

- **Destructive** – relates to improvements which are needed and is often given in a negative way which could demoralise the learner.

- **Objective** – clearly relates to specific assessment requirements and is factual regarding what has and has not been met.

- **Subjective** – often just a personal opinion; which can be biased, for example if the assessor is friendly with the learner. Feedback might be vague and not based on the assessment requirements.

When giving feedback to learners you need to be aware that it could affect their self-esteem and whether they continue with the programme or not. The quality of feedback received can be a key factor towards their progress, and their ability to learn new knowledge and skills. Ongoing constructive feedback which is developmental and has been carefully thought through is an indication of your interest in your learner, and of your intention to help them develop and do well in the future.

When giving feedback:

- Own your statements by beginning with the word 'I' rather than 'You' (however, written feedback could be given in the third person if your organisation prefers).

- Start with something positive, for example: 'I really liked the confident manner in which you delivered your presentation.'

- Be specific about what you have seen, for example: 'I felt the way you explained that topic was really interesting due to your knowledge and humour,' or, 'I found the way you explained that topic was rather confusing to me.'

- Offer constructive and specific follow-on points, for example: 'I feel I would have understood it better if you had broken the subject down into smaller stages.'

- End with something positive or developmental, for example: 'I enjoyed your presentation – you had prepared well and came across as very organised and professional,' or, 'I enjoyed your session; however, issuing a handout summarising the key points would be really helpful to refer to after the session.'

Being constructive, specific and developmental with what you say, and owning your statements by beginning with the word 'I' should help your learner focus upon what you are saying, and listen to how they can improve. If you don't have any follow-on points then don't create them just for the sake of it. Conversely, if you do have any negative points or criticisms, don't say, 'My only negative point is . . .' or, 'My only criticisms are . . .' It's much better to replace these words and say, 'Some areas for development could be . . .' instead.

Using the Saucier *(2001)* SARA model can lead to the recipient of the feedback going through the following four processes associated with change: **S**hock, **A**nger, **R**esistance and **A**cceptance. Over the years, some other words have been used. For example, instead of shock: surprise; instead of anger: annoyance or anxiety; instead of resistance: rejection.

Example

Suraya had marked an assignment from one of her learners, Jenna, who had not fully met all the requirements. Jenna had been progressing well with all her other assignments so far. When Suraya gave verbal feedback to Jenna, she found she was initially shocked that she had not passed, then angry, saying that Suraya must have made a mistake when marking. When Suraya explained what Jenna needed to do to meet the requirements, Jenna initially resisted, but then accepted that she hadn't met all the requirements.

This example shows how a learner went through the four processes of SARA. At some point you might find your learners doing the same. However, don't take it personally. Providing you have assessed correctly, your learner will have to accept that they need to do further work if they wish to achieve.

You might need to give feedback to other people, for example your learner's supervisor in their work environment. You need to be careful of what you say and how you say it. It could be that your feedback might be used as part of the staff appraisal process to monitor your learner's performance and job prospects.

Analysing learner achievement

At some point, you might need to analyse your learners' achievements, perhaps for statistical and audit purposes. This could be by comparing your learners' results to benchmark figures, targets, or by comparing learners' achievements to each other or different cohorts of learners.

Norm-referencing

If you want to compare the achievements of a group of learners against one another, you could use norm-referencing, which is a form of grading in addition to marking. Grading is when you give an A, B or C, whereas marking is whether they pass or not. Grading and marking go together when required; for example, a GCSE grade 2 is still a pass mark (where U is fail and 9 is the highest grade).

Norm-referencing will proportion your grades accordingly, as there will always be those in your group who will achieve a high grade, and those who will achieve a low grade, leaving the rest in the middle. You would allocate grades according to a quota; for example, the top 20 per cent would achieve an A, the next 20 per cent a B, and so on. Norm-referencing uses the achievement of a group to set the standards for specific grades, or for how many learners will pass or fail. This type of assessment is useful to maintain consistency of results over time; whether the test questions are easy or hard, there will always be those achieving a high grade or a lower grade.

Example

Joan has a group of 25 learners who have just taken a test consisting of 20 questions. She wants to allocate grades A to E to her group. She has worked out the top 20 per cent will achieve an A, the second 20 per cent a B and so on. When she marks the tests, she is surprised to see the lowest mark is 16 out of 20, meaning a grade E. Even though the learners have done well in the test, they are still given a low grade in comparison to the rest of the group.

A fairer method would have been to just set a pass mark, for example 15 out of 20, and not use grading at all. Learners achieving 14 or below could be referred and retake a different test at a later date.

Criterion-referencing

Criterion-referencing enables learners to achieve based upon their own merit, as their achievements are not compared with one another. All learners therefore have equality of opportunity. If grades are allocated, for example a distinction, credit or pass, there will be specific criteria which must have been met for each. These criteria are usually supplied by the awarding organisation if learners are taking an accredited qualification.

Example

Pass – *described the activity.*

Credit – *described and analysed the activity.*

Distinction – *described, analysed and critically reflected upon the activity.*

Some qualifications may simply be assessed as a pass or a fail, such as a multiple-choice test where learners must achieve 7 out of 10 for a pass. However, learners with excellent subject knowledge or occupational competence can often fail online tests or multiple-choice tests because they don't understand the process. Online multiple-choice tests are a very effective, instant and low-cost way to test learners, but because learners can perceive them as quick and easy they might have a tendency not to read the questions properly.

Sometimes, negative marking can be used, whereby a mark is deducted for every incorrect answer. You may need to seek advice when using this type of assessment.

If learners are eligible to retake a test, it's advisable to leave a period of time, for example seven days, before they take it again. If learners are taking a test that other learners have already attempted, you need to ensure they do not have access to others' responses. If learners feel the urge to cheat, they are ultimately only cheating themselves. A bank of questions would be useful; this way you could choose a certain number of random questions that will always be different. Computer-generated question papers should automatically choose different questions for different learners and tests.

Results analysis

If you assess a programme which requires grades to be given to learners in addition to marking, you will need to analyse the results regarding their achievements. The grades could be expressed as:

- 1, 2, 3, 4, 5
- A, B, C, D, E
- achieved/not achieved
- competent/not yet competent
- distinction, credit, pass, fail
- pass, refer, fail

- percentages, e.g. 80 per cent

- satisfactory, good, outstanding.

Analysing the results will help you see not only how well your learners have done, but whether or not there are any trends. For example, if all your learners received an average of C, but another assessor's group achieved an average of B, is there a fault on your part?

If you had a group of 30 learners who all achieved an A grade, was this due to your excellent support, the skills and knowledge of your learners, or by your being too lenient when assessing? Having sample answers to compare your learners' responses to will help you remain objective.

If you had a group of 15 learners who all failed an assignment, you could ask yourself the same questions. However, it could be that the assignment questions were worded in a con-fusing way, or you had given them the assignment too early in the programme. If most of your group averaged a grade of 50 per cent, whereas a colleague's group averaged 80 per cent, was this because you had given your learners misleading or ambiguous information relating to that topic?

Asking yourself these questions will help you ascertain if you are producing assessments that are fit for purpose; if not, you will need to do something about it. For example, you may need to amend your teaching or assessment methods, reword your questions or redesign some assessment activities.

Extension Activity

If you are currently assessing, analyse your learners' achievements for the past year. For example, compile statistics relating to how many learners commenced, how many completed, and in what timeframe. If you are assessing work which is graded, analyse the grades over a period of time and see if there are any issues or trends. If you are assessing towards a funded qualification, you could compare your learners' achievements with those of national success rates. This information can be found on the Skills Funding Agency (SFA) website (www. gov.uk/government/organisations/skills-funding-agency).

Reviewing learner progress

It is important to review the progress of your learners, to know not only how they are progressing and what they have achieved, but what they may need to do to improve. It also gives you the opportunity to discuss any concerns they may have. Reviews of progress with learners on an individual basis can form part of the assessment process, and could provide the opportunity to carry out formative assessments in an informal way. They also give your learner the opportunity to ask questions they might have been self-conscious about asking in a group situation.

The review process should be carried out at a suitable time during the learning and assessment process. Reviews can be part of individual tutorials or one-to-one discussions, and records should always be maintained. Informal reviews and discussions can take place at any opportune time. Reviewing progress enables you to differentiate effectively, ensuring that the needs of your learners are met, and that they are being challenged to develop to their full potential. If learners are taking a higher-level qualification, you should be giving them more autonomy towards their achievement, i.e. not giving them the same amount of support as a learner taking a lower-level qualification. The review process also helps ascertain if learners are experiencing any difficulties, enabling you to arrange for any necessary support or further training.

Activity

Consider the advantages of reviewing a learner's progress from your point of view as an assessor. Make a list and then compare it to the following bullet points.

Reviewing learner progress enables you to:

- ascertain any learner issues or concerns

- confirm progress and achievements

- plan areas for further development

- check skills and knowledge gained from a previous session, before commencing the current session

- discuss any confidential or sensitive issues

- give constructive and developmental feedback

- keep a record of what was discussed

- involve your learner, formally or informally

- involve your learner's employers and witnesses (if applicable) to gain more information about their progress and achievements

- motivate your learner

- plan for differentiation

- plan future learning and assessments

- plan more challenging or creative assessment opportunities

- provide opportunities for further learning, development and/or support

- review your own contribution to the learning and assessment process

- revise your delivery and assessment materials

- revise your strategies for assessment

- update your learner's action plan or assessment plan.

If possible, a formal one-to-one review should take place at some point during every programme, as it can be a key aspect of the assessment process.

Example

Richard has a group of 12 learners who are attending a weekly evening class in pottery skills from 7 to 9 p.m. for three terms. He has decided to dedicate one session every term for individual tutorials and reviews of progress. While he is carrying these out, the rest of the group will work on projects or use the organisation's library and computer facilities. This enables Richard to discuss individual progress, concerns and action points with each learner. It also helps him evaluate the assessment process.

If there is no set review or tutorial procedure, or you are not required to review your learners' progress, it would still be a useful activity if you have the time. The review process should be ongoing until your learner has completed the programme, even if it is carried out on an informal basis. Regular reviews can help to keep your learners motivated, make them feel less isolated, and appreciate how they are progressing. It is also an opportunity for your learners to contribute to the assessment process by voicing their views and discussing any concerns they may have.

When assessing and reviewing progress, always try to ensure that the environment meets your learners' basic needs, such as feeling safe and comfortable. This will enable them to feel secure enough to discuss things with you, and to be motivated to continue.

Maslow (1987) introduced the concept of a *hierarchy of needs* in 1954 after rejecting the idea that human behaviour was determined by childhood events. He argued that there are five needs which represent different levels of motivation which must be met. Figure 4.1 shows the needs expressed in educational terms, in relation to learning. The highest level is *self-actualising*, meaning people are fully functional, possess a healthy personality, and take responsibility for themselves and their actions. In educational terms this can mean they are achieving what they wanted to. Maslow also believed that people should be able to move through these needs to the highest level, providing that they are given an education that promotes growth.

Ensuring the review and assessment environments meet your learners' first-level needs will enable them to feel comfortable and secure enough to learn and progress to the higher levels. You will need to appreciate that some learners may not have these lower needs met in their home lives, making it difficult for them to move on to the higher levels throughout their learning. Therefore, if you can ensure the environment is suitable, not too hot or too cold, and that learners can have a break for refreshments, this should help the learning process.

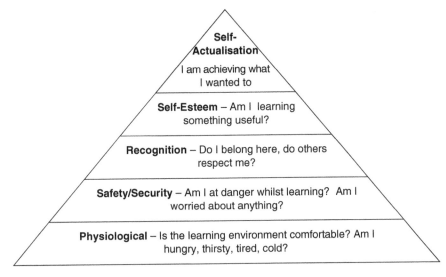

Figure 4.1 Maslow's hierarchy of needs expressed in educational terms

The review process should involve:

- arranging a suitable date, time and location, and confirming these with your learner

- communicating with anyone else involved in the assessment process

- obtaining in advance all relevant records relating to your learner, the subject and the assessments carried out

- discussing any issues or concerns, progress and achievements so far

- updating the action plan or assessment plan with achievements and dates

- identifying any training needs

- planning future assessment activities and targets, along with the next review date

- signing and dating the review record and giving a copy to your learner.

Always listen to what your learners have to say, without interrupting them; they may not have the opportunity elsewhere to talk to someone about sensitive issues. If they don't respond immediately, pause and let them think in silence for a moment rather than pressuring them with further questions. Ensure the confidentiality of any information your learners disclose to you, otherwise you could lose their trust and respect. However, you need to know where your boundaries as an assessor lie, and not get involved personally. There are exceptions, for example if you have any cause for concern as to your learner's safety. If you suspect bullying or radicalisation, then you must pass this information on to whoever is responsible for safeguarding.

If you have groups of learners, you could carry out a group review. At an appropriate time during the programme, you could hold a discussion regarding how they feel their learning is progressing. This is particularly useful when you need to assess group activities. It could be that some activities do not suit the learning preferences of a few learners, therefore not enabling them to contribute fully. Using several different activities could alleviate this problem, and make the process more interesting. Feedback from group reviews can inform the assessment planning process, and also be a valuable tool to evaluate the programme as a whole.

Extension Activity

Find out what the procedure is for reviewing learners' progress and/or holding tutorials, either one to one or in groups. Carry out a review with a learner and try to follow the process in the previous bullet-point list. What was the process like from your perspective as an assessor, and from your learner's perspective? What could you improve and why?

Record keeping

It is important to keep records; otherwise, how can you prove what progress your learners have made and know exactly what they have achieved? You also need to satisfy any company, quality assurance, awarding organisation or regulatory authorities' audit requirements. This will usually be for a set period, for example three years, and should be the original records, not photocopies or carbon copies. It is fine to give copies to your learners, as it is harder to forge a copy than an original. Sadly, there are learners who do this; therefore keeping the originals will ensure your records are authentic.

When learners submit work, such as an assignment, it is good practice to issue a receipt. If not, a learner might say that they have submitted their work when they haven't.

Keeping full and accurate factual records is necessary in case one of your learners appeals against an assessment decision you have made. If this happens, don't take it personally – they will be appealing against your decision, not you as a person. You will also need to pass records to your internal quality assurer if necessary, and any other authorised colleagues who have an interest in your learner's progress and achievement.

Table 4.3 lists examples of assessment records which you might need to complete or maintain; however, you might not use all of them, depending upon your job role. Some other records might be maintained centrally within your organisation using an electronic management information system. For example:

- assessor details: name, contact information, curriculum vitae, continuing professional development (CPD) plans and records

- awarding organisation's qualification specification

- enrolment, registration and/or and unique learner numbers

- equal opportunities data such as an analysis of learners by ethnic origin, disability, gender and age

- evaluation forms, questionnaire and survey results

- internal and external quality assurance reports

- learner details: name, address, date of birth, contact information, registration numbers, photo identification

- organisational self-assessment report and records of actions taken

- regulatory and funding guidance.

Table 4.3 Examples of assessment records

Assessment records	
<ul><li>achievement dates and grades</li><li>action plans</li><li>appeals and complaints records</li><li>application forms</li><li>assessment plan and review records</li><li>assessment tracking sheet showing progression of all learners</li><li>authentication declarations/statements</li><li>checklists</li><li>copies of certificates</li><li>diagnostic test results</li><li>employer name and contact details (if applicable)</li><li>formative and summative records</li><li>feedback records</li><li>initial assessment results</li></ul>	<ul><li>interview and enrolment records</li><li>job description, if work based</li><li>learning preference results</li><li>observation checklists</li><li>observation reports</li><li>professional discussion records</li><li>progress reports</li><li>receipts for submitted work</li><li>records of achievement</li><li>records of oral questions and responses</li><li>retention, achievement and destination records</li><li>schemes of work and session plans</li><li>standardisation records</li><li>tutorial reviews</li><li>witness testimonies</li></ul>

There might be a standardised approach to completing your records, for example the amount of detail which must be added, or whether the records should be completed manually or electronically. You will need to find out what your organisation expects you to do. Some organisations now use handheld devices to input assessment information directly. These can also be used to support learners to produce their work electronically, such as in creating an e-portfolio of evidence towards a qualification.

Activity

Find out what records you are required to maintain, where you can access them and how they should be completed, i.e. the amount of information required. How long must they be kept at your organisation, where should they be kept, and can they be completed manually or electronically, or both?

All records should be accurate and legible. If you need to make any amendments manually, make crossings out rather than use correction fluid, or save a different version electronically. Try to keep up to date with your administrative work, even if this is carried out electronically. If you leave it a while, you may forget to note important points. You will need to be organised and have a system; learner records could be stored alphabetically in a filing cabinet, or in separate electronic folders on a computer. If storing electronically, make sure you keep a back-up copy in case anything gets deleted accidentally. Other records could be stored by the programme or qualification title, or the awarding organisation name.

Example

Andreas has a group of 12 learners working towards a Certificate in Health and Social Care. As he travels around various workplaces to carry out assessment, he maintains an A4 lever arch file, which has a tracking sheet at the front to record the dates of each learner's completed units. He then has plastic wallets for each learner, filed alphabetically, which contain their assessment plans, review records, and feedback and action records. As he manually completes a document, he makes a carbon copy to give to his learners. Andreas's organisation will be moving over to a web-based electronic storage system in the next few months, which will make it quicker to access the information, providing there is an internet connection.

When completing any records, if signatures are required these should be obtained as soon as possible after the event, if they cannot be obtained on the day. Any signatures added later should have the date they were added, rather than the date the form was originally completed. If you are assessing your learners directly, for example by an observation, you will know who they are. If you are assessing work that has been handed to you on a different date, or sent electronically, you will need to ensure it is the work of your learner, perhaps by checking their identification. If you are completing documents electronically, you will need to find out what the policy is in your organisation as to whether an email address or electronic signature is required or not. It could be that one document is signed by all parties at the beginning or end of the programme, instead of each separate document. This would confirm their identity, and verify that work was all their own.

Record keeping and ensuring the authenticity of your learners' work is of paramount importance. To satisfy everyone involved in the assessment process you must be able to show a valid audit trail for all your decisions. If assessment decisions count towards the achievement of a qualification, it is crucial to keep your feedback records, along with any action identified for each learner. Records must always be kept safe and secure; your car boot or home is not a good idea, nor is a corner of the staffroom or an open-plan office. Awarding organisations expect records to be securely managed, whether they are manual or electronic.

A useful method to record overall learner achievement is known as an assessment tracking sheet. Table 4.4 is an example of a completed tracking sheet for five learners, each working towards five units of a qualification. It shows the dates and grades and is a method of seeing the achievement of all learners at a glance. For the purpose of future-proofing this textbook, a year has not been added to the dates. Assessors should add the year as well as the day and month to any records which are completed.

Table 4.4 Example assessment tracking sheet

Assessment tracking sheet					
Assessor: Jenny Smith	**Qualification:** Level 1 Certificate in Hospitality and Catering				
Learner name and registration number	**Aspects assessed**				
	101	102	103	104	105
Chang Hanadi 4524UDBQ	11 June Pass		8 March Pass	10 May Refer 15 May Pass	
Hamed Aamir 1674UEME		7 May Pass			
Jones Irene 1234ABCD	6 Feb Pass				
Wilson Peter 7985IENF	15 Jan Pass	4 Feb Pass			
Young Lou 7496UWME	10 Jan Pass				

RARPA records

If you are assessing a programme which is not accredited by an awarding organisation, you may need to follow the requirements for **R**ecognising **A**nd **R**ecording **P**rogress and **A**chievement in non-accredited learning (RARPA). There are five processes to RARPA.

- **Aims** – these should be appropriate to the individual or group of learners.

- **Initial assessment** – this should be used to establish each learner's starting point.

- **Identification of appropriately challenging learning objectives** – these should be agreed, renegotiated and revised as necessary after formative assessment, and should be appropriate to each learner.

- **Recognition and recording of progress and achievement during the programme** – this should include assessor feedback, learner reflection and reviews of progress.

- **End of programme** – this includes summative assessment, learner self-assessment and a review of overall progress and achievement. This should be in relation to the learning objectives and any other outcomes achieved during the programme.

If you use the RARPA system, you will need to check what records must be maintained; there may be a standard system for you to follow or you may need to design your own assessment records.

Legislation relating to records

All records should be securely kept and should only be accessible by relevant staff. You need to ensure that you comply with organisational and statutory guidelines such as the Data Protection Act (1998) and the Freedom of Information Act (2000).

The Data Protection Act (1998) is mandatory for all organisations that hold or process personal data. The Act contains eight principles, to ensure that data is:

- processed fairly and lawfully

- obtained and used only for specified and lawful purposes

- adequate, relevant and not excessive

- accurate and, where necessary, kept up to date

- kept for no longer than necessary

- processed in accordance with the individual's rights

- kept secure

- transferred only to countries that offer adequate protection.

The Freedom of Information Act (2000) gives your learners the opportunity to request to see the information public authorities hold about them. All external stakeholders, such as awarding organisations and funding bodies, should be aware of your systems of record keeping, as they may need to approve certain records or storage systems. Confidentiality should be maintained regarding all information you keep.

Extension Activity

Find out who else will need access to your assessment records and why. How can you ensure you are following legislation such as the Data Protection Act (1998) and Freedom of Information Act (2000)? What other legislation, codes of practice and policies must you be aware of regarding keeping records?

Summary

Knowing how to make a valid assessment decision, and giving constructive and developmental feedback to your learners, should help motivate them to progress and achieve. Maintaining adequate records will ensure you are compliant with all relevant assessment requirements, and show an audit trail of learners' progress and achievements.

You might like to carry out further research by accessing the books and websites listed at the end of this chapter.

This chapter has covered the following topics:

- Making assessment decisions
- Providing feedback
- Reviewing learner progress
- Record keeping

References and further information

Boud, D. and Molloy, E. (2012) *Feedback in Higher and Professional Education: Understanding it and Doing it Well*. Abingdon: Routledge.

Maslow, A. (1987) *Motivation and Personality* (3rd revised edn). New York: Pearson Education.

Murphy, P. (1999) *Learners, Learning and Assessment*. London: Paul Chapman Publishing.

Read, H. (2011) *The Best Assessor's Guide*. Bideford: Read On Publications.

Reece, I. and Walker, S. (2007) *Teaching, Training and Learning: A Practical Guide* (6th edn). Sunderland: Business Education Publishers.

Saucier, G. et al. (2001) *Beyond Compliance: Building a Corporate Governance Culture*. Joint Committee on Corporate Governance.

Tummons, J. (2011) *Assessing Learning in the Lifelong Learning Sector* (3rd edn). Exeter: Learning Matters.

Websites

Association for Achievement and Improvement through Assessment (AAIA) – **www.aaia.org.uk**

Chartered Institute of Educational Assessors – **www.ciea.org.uk**

Copyright, Designs and Patents Act (1988) – **www.legislation.gov.uk/ukpga/1988/48/contents**

Data Protection Act – **www.legislation.gov.uk/ukpga/1998/29/contents**

Freedom of Information Act – **www.legislation.gov.uk/ukpga/2000/36/contents**

Oxford Learning Institute: Giving and receiving feedback – **www.learning.ox.ac.uk/supervision/stages/feedback/**

RARPA – **www.learningcurve.org.uk/resources/learning/rarpa**

Skills Funding Agency (SFA) – **www.gov.uk/government/organisations/skills-funding-agency**

5 QUALITY ASSURANCE OF ASSESSMENT

Introduction

Quality assurance should take place to ensure the products and services your learners access are the best they can be. The *product* is the programme, qualification or set of standards that the learner is working towards. The *service* is everything which underpins the product and supports the learner. If quality assurance does not take place, there could be risks to the accuracy, consistency and fairness of assessment practice, which might disadvantage the learners. Quality assurance should be a continual process with the aim of maintaining and improving the products and services offered.

This chapter will explore the various aspects of quality assuring the assessment process.

This chapter will cover the following topics:

- Standardising practice
- Internal quality assurance
- External quality assurance
- Appeals, complaints and disputes

Standardising practice

Standardisation of practice ensures reliability and fairness regarding assessment planning, decisions and feedback. This should enable a consistent experience for all learners from the time they commence to the time they achieve or leave. You should standardise your decisions and the way you complete your records with other assessors, particularly where more than one assessor is involved in the same subject area. It is also an opportunity to ensure all assessors are interpreting the qualification and assessment requirements accurately. Standardisation enables people to work as a team rather than on their own, and to give an equitable service to all learners.

Assessors need to take into account the individual needs of their learners, and the settings in which assessment takes place. For example, if a learner is being assessed in a health and social care setting with a client, it might be more appropriate to obtain a reflective account or a witness testimony. An observation carried out by an assessor could upset the client in this situation. Therefore, the number of observations or pieces of evidence from different learners for the same aspect of a qualification could differ. Unless there are written requirements as to the type of evidence and number of observations required, assessors can make their own decisions depending upon the situation.

Activity

Find out when the next standardisation event will take place, along with what activities will be carried out. Prior to this, ensure that you are fully familiar with what is going to be standardised. Think of some questions to ask your colleagues regarding what you are assessing, and the planning and feedback process.

Benefits of standardisation

The main benefit is that standardisation gives a consistent experience for all learners, no matter who their assessor is. It's also a good way of maintaining professional development, and ensuring compliance and accountability with awarding organisations and regulatory authorities' requirements.

Other benefits include:

- an opportunity to discuss changes and developments
- assessment decisions are fair for all learners
- clearly defined roles and responsibilities
- compliance with relevant codes of practice and regulations
- confirmation of own practice
- consistency and fairness of judgements and decisions
- empowerment of teachers, trainers and assessors
- giving staff the time to meet formally
- maintaining an audit trail of what has been standardised
- meeting quality assurance requirements
- reassessment to spot errors or incorrect decisions by assessors, or even plagiarism or cheating by learners
- setting action plans for the development of assessment activities
- sharing of good practice
- spotting trends or inconsistencies
- succession planning if staff are likely to leave
- upholding the credibility of the delivery and assessment process and practice.

Attending a standardisation event will give you the opportunity to share good practice and to compare your assessment decisions with those of your colleagues, by looking at their assessed work and vice versa. You can then discuss your findings as a team. This will ensure you have interpreted the requirements accurately, that the learner evidence is appropriate and that the assessment records are completed correctly. Even if you don't learn anything new, it will hopefully confirm you are doing things correctly.

Standardisation events are not team meetings; the latter are to discuss issues relating to the management of the programme, for example awarding organisation updates, targets, success rates and learner issues.

Standardisation events can be held to:

- compare how documents and records have been completed

- create schemes of work, session plans and course materials

- design or revise assessment and quality assurance documents

- discuss decisions made by other assessors

- discuss the qualification/programme requirements

- interpret policies and procedures

- prepare materials for induction and initial assessments

- prepare assessment activities, e.g. questions and expected responses.

If you assess a vocational qualification, you might decide to carry out three observations with each of your learners and give them a written test, whereas another assessor might only carry out one observation and ask some oral questions. Standardising this approach between all assessors ensures the process is fair. There are times when an individual learner's needs should be taken into account, which will lead to a difference in assessment activities. However, all learners should be entitled to the same assessment experience, no matter which assessor they have been allocated. Table 5.1 opposite gives an example of a completed template used by assessors for standardising assessed work.

Example

Jon was a new assessor, and was not very familiar with the standards of the qualification he was due to assess. The full team of assessors met once a month to discuss the content of each unit. This ensured they were all interpreting the requirements in the same way and making correct decisions. Jon attended the next meeting and was given the opportunity to reassess a unit which had already been assessed by someone else. This activity helped him understand the requirements and to see how the documentation was completed.

Other standardisation activities can include:

- creating assessment materials, assignments and recommended answers

- new staff shadowing experienced staff

- peer observations and feedback to ensure consistency of practice

Table 5.1 Example standardisation record for assessed work

Standardisation record for assessed work			
Learner: Ann Bex			Original assessor: J. Smith
Qualification/unit: Level 2 Customer Service			Standardising assessor: M. Singh
Aspect/s standardised: Unit 101 evidence and assessment records			Date: 16 February
Checklist	Yes	No	Comments/Action required
Is there an agreed assessment plan with SMART targets?	Y		Your plan had very clear SMART targets with realistic dates for achievement.
Which methods were used? Are the assessment methods appropriate and sufficient?	Y		Observation, questioning, products and witness testimonies have been used. You could reduce the number of observations in the workplace if you can rely on the witness testimonies.
Does the evidence meet ALL the required criteria?	Y		All assessment criteria have been met through the various assessment methods.
Does the evidence meet VACSR?	Y		You have ensured all these points; you also took into consideration an aspect that you hadn't planned to assess, but that naturally occurred during an observation.
Is there a feedback record clearly showing what has been achieved? (Is it adequate and developmental?)	Y		Your feedback is very thorough and confirms your learner's achievements. However, you could be more developmental to guide your learner towards ways of improving her current practice.
Has subsequent action been identified? (if applicable)		N	The feedback record showed what had been achieved and what feedback had been given. However, no further action had been identified. You need to plan which units will be assessed next and set target dates for their achievement.
Do you agree with the assessment decision?	Y		I agree with the decision you made; however, I do feel you could have reduced the number of workplace observations.
Are all relevant documents signed and dated (including countersignatures if applicable)?		N	As you are still working towards your assessor award, you need to ensure that your decisions have been countersigned by a qualified assessor.
Are original assessment records stored separately from the learner's work?		N	You have given your original copies to your learner; you need to ensure that you keep the original and give your learner a copy. The original can be kept manually or electronically but must be kept secure for three years in the assessor office.

General comments:

Although there are a few Ns in the checklist, this does not affect my judgement as I agree with your decision for this learner. You agreed a SMART assessment plan with your learner which was followed through with assessment and feedback. All your records are in place; however, don't forget to keep originals in the office and give your learner a copy. This is part of our organisation policy due to some learners having amended the original copy in their favour. It's harder to amend a copy as the pen colour is more prominent.

Make sure you set clear targets for future development and assessment opportunities when you give feedback. It's better to do it at this point, while you are with your learner, to enable a two-way conversation to take place and to agree suitable target dates.

As you are still working towards your assessor award, you need to ensure your decisions have been countersigned by a qualified assessor. Please do this by the end of the month.

Comments from original assessor in response to the above:

I agree with your feedback. I had forgotten about keeping original copies and only giving a photocopy to my learner. I will ensure I do this in future. I wasn't able to get hold of my countersignatory as he was on holiday, but I will make sure he reads my records and signs them upon his return. I will then take a copy ready to use as evidence for my assessor award. I realise that I must give more developmental feedback and agree future targets when I am with my learner.

Key: SMART: specific, measurable, achievable, relevant, timebound
VACSR: valid, authentic, current, sufficient, reliable

- role-play activities such as assessment planning, making a decision, giving feedback, dealing with a complaint

- internal quality assurers agreeing how their practice will be consistent to support their assessors.

Records should be maintained of all standardisation activities and any identified actions, which should be acted upon. An external quality assurer will want to view the records, if it's applicable to the qualification.

It's important to keep up to date with any changes regarding what you are assessing; for example, if you are assessing an accredited qualification, the content will be revised every few years. Awarding organisations issue regular updates, either by hard copy or electronically. Once you receive these, you need to discuss the content with your colleagues to ensure that you all interpret them in the same way, perhaps during a team meeting.

Using technology for standardisation purposes

Technology can be used for standardisation activities and is ideal if not all the team members can attend a meeting or activity at the same time, or they are located in different buildings.

When standardising the decisions assessors have made based on electronic evidence, it's important to be sure the work does belong to the learner, and that the assessor has confirmed the authenticity of it.

Some examples of using technology for standardisation activities include:

- holding meetings via Skype or videoconferencing facilities to discuss the interpretation of aspects of a programme or qualification

- using online webinars to help standardise delivery and assessment approaches

- creating, updating and sharing documents online, e.g. schemes of work, session plans and course materials

- taking digital recordings or videos of role-play activities or case studies, e.g. assessor decisions, and giving developmental feedback; assessors could view them remotely to comment on strengths and limitations of a particular method

- making visual recordings of how to complete forms and reports; if a staff member is unsure how to fill in a form they could access a video to see an example

- recording standardisation activities and uploading them to an intranet or virtual learning environment (VLE) for viewing/listening to later.

Extension Activity

Find out what activities are used for standardisation purposes, and the types of records used to document them. Have a look at Table 5.1 on page 127 to see if it compares to anything you use. Consider how you could carry out some standardisation activities using technology.

Internal quality assurance

Internal quality assurance (IQA) relates to monitoring the process your learner goes through during their time with you. It also includes monitoring the training and assessment activities, which are a substantial part of the IQA process. Internal *verification* was the previous term used for monitoring assessment; however, IQA monitors the whole process, from when a learner commences to when they finish, i.e. the full learner journey.

If IQA does not take place, there could be risks to the accuracy, consistency and fairness of assessment practice. This could lead to incorrect decisions and ultimately disadvantage the learners.

Quality *assurance* is different from quality *control* and quality *improvement*. Quality assurance aims to avoid problems, stabilise, and improve products and services by monitoring what takes place on an ongoing basis. Quality control aims to find problems at the conclusion of the products or services used. Quality improvement aims to raise the quality of the products and services by comparing what has happened with what will happen. If there isn't a quality system in place, it could lead to complacency by the staff involved, as they might perceive that what they are doing is acceptable, when it might not be.

Example

Huw will quality assure an accredited qualification by observing his assessors with their learners, and sampling their work. The IQA process is therefore of a product. However, Huw will also monitor the support his assessors provide to their learners: the service. He will do this throughout the time the learners are taking the qualification. If he used a system of quality control, he would only check what has occurred at the end of the programme, when the learner had completed the qualification. This would not allow any changes to take place if any problems or issues had been identified. While Huw is not in a position to change the product (the qualification), he would like to improve the service the learners receive in future, based on what he has monitored in the past.

Usually, internal quality assurers are also experienced assessors in the subject area they are quality assuring. For example, if the subject area is retail, they should not be internally quality assuring other subjects they are not experienced in, such as hairdressing. The process might be the same for each subject, but the internal quality assurer must be fully familiar with the assessment criteria to confirm the assessor's decision. If you are quality assuring an accredited qualification, you will need to read the assessment strategy from the awarding organisation. This will state whether or not you must also be a qualified assessor in the same subject that you will internally quality assure.

Roles and responsibilities of an internal quality assurer

The main role is to carry out the IQA process according to the qualification requirements, or those of the programme, standards, criteria or job specification being assessed.

This might include:

- advising, supporting and providing developmental feedback to assessors

- documenting the quality assurance strategy, process and decisions

- ensuring assessors interpret, understand and consistently apply the correct standards and requirements

- identifying issues and trends, for example, if several learners are misinterpreting the same topic

- leading standardisation activities to ensure the accuracy and consistency of assessment decisions between assessors

- monitoring the full learner journey from commencement to completion

- planning and carrying out the sampling of assessed work

- taking part in continuing professional development (CPD)

- talking to learners, assessors and other relevant staff

- working towards relevant IQA qualifications.

Often IQAs are supervisors or managers and are naturally responsible for staff, systems and procedures. Some are still working as assessors and performing both roles. That's absolutely fine as long as they are not responsible for the quality assurance of their own assessment decisions, as that would be a conflict of interest. Some smaller organisations might only have one assessor and one internal quality assurer, which again is fine providing they remain fully objective when carrying out their role. In some small teams, with perhaps one assessor and one internal quality assurer, they can swap roles and review each other's assessment decisions. Again, it's not a problem unless the awarding organisation deems it is. It could be considered a good way of standardising practice, as each will be monitoring the other regularly to ensure consistency.

Internal quality assurers might also be required to:

- analyse enrolment, retention, achievement and progression data

- carry out a training needs analysis with assessors

- compile self-assessment reports

- countersign other internal quality assurers' judgements

- deal with appeals and complaints

- design advertising and marketing materials

- design, issue and analyse questionnaires and surveys, and set action plans based on the findings

- ensure qualifications are fit for purpose and validated by the organisation as being appropriate for learners and local employment requirements

- ensure strategies, policies and procedures are regularly reviewed

- facilitate appropriate staff development, training and CPD

- induct and mentor new staff, support existing staff and carry out staff appraisals

- interview and induct new staff

- liaise with others involved in the IQA process, e.g. trainers, witnesses from the workplace and external quality assurers

- prepare agendas and chair meetings

- prepare for external inspections and visits, and liaise with administrative staff

- implement any action and improvement points from reports

- provide statistics and reports to line managers

- register and certificate learners with an awarding organisation

- set targets and/or performance indicators.

The IQA process

Internal quality assurance should be carried out from commencement to the completion of the product or service. If there is no external formal examination taken by learners, there has to be a system of monitoring the performance of assessors. If not, assessors might make incorrect judgements or pass a learner who hasn't met all the requirements, perhaps because they are biased towards them, or have made a mistake. Assessment and IQA systems should be monitored and evaluated continuously to identify any action and improvement points, which should then be implemented. This also includes the continuing CPD of assessors and other internal quality assurers.

An internal quality assurer must be appointed to carry out the quality role within an organisation where there are assessment activities taking place.

As a minimum, the internal quality assurer should:

- plan what will be monitored, from whom and when

- observe trainer and assessor performance and provide developmental feedback

- sample assessment records, learners' work and assessor decisions

- meet with learners and others, for example witnesses from the workplace

- facilitate the standardisation of assessor practice

- support assessors.

If there is more than one internal quality assurer for a particular subject area, one person should take the lead role and co-ordinate the others. All internal quality assurers should standardise their practice with each other to ensure they interpret the requirements in the same way.

Activity

> Obtain a copy of the qualification specification for your subject, or the relevant criteria that will be internally quality assured. If you are currently an assessor you should already have a copy. Familiarise yourself with the assessment strategy and the requirements for IQA. Consider what aspects of the assessment process will be quality assured and why.

The internal quality assurance cycle

Depending upon the subject, the IQA cycle will usually be followed as in Figure 5.1. The cycle will continue to ensure the assessment process is constantly monitored and improved if necessary.

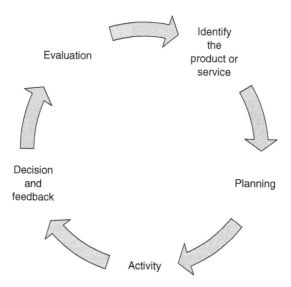

Figure 5.1 The internal quality assurance (IQA) cycle

The IQA cycle involves the following aspects:

- **Identify the product or service** – ascertain what is to be assessed and internally quality assured and why. For example, are learners working towards a qualification or are staff being observed performing their job roles? The criteria will need to be clear, i.e. units from a qualification, standards, criteria or aspects of a job specification. Learners should be allocated to assessors in a fair way: for example, according to location or workload.

- **Planning** – devise a sample plan to arrange what will be monitored, from whom and when. Plan the dates to observe assessor performance, and to hold team meetings and standardisation events. Information will need to be obtained from assessors to assist the planning process, and risks taken into account such as assessor knowledge, qualifications and experience.

- **Activity** – carry out activities such as sampling learners' work, observing trainer and assessor performance, and sampling assessment records and decisions. This also includes holding meetings and standardisation events, supporting and training assessors and communicating with others involved in the assessment and IQA process.

- **Decision and feedback** – make a judgement as to whether or not the assessor has performed satisfactorily and made valid and reliable decisions. Provide developmental feedback as to what was good or what could be improved. Agree action points if necessary and follow them up.

- **Evaluation** – review the whole process of assessment and IQA to determine what could be improved or done differently. Agree action plans if necessary; implement and follow them up. Follow any action plans from external quality assurers or others involved in the IQA process. Write self-assessment reports as necessary.

The cycle will then begin again, with an identification of what needs to be monitored and when. Throughout the cycle, standardisation of practice between internal quality assurers should take place; this will help ensure the consistency and fairness of decisions. Feedback should also be obtained from learners and others involved in the assessment process. You will find details of how to do this in Chapter 6. Records must be maintained of all activities for audit requirements. All staff should maintain their CPD and follow legal and organisational requirements. If the qualification is accredited by an awarding organisation, external quality assurance will also take place.

Extension Activity

Look at the cycle in Figure 5.1 and note down all the activities an IQA should carry out for each aspect. As an assessor, would you make any changes to your practice as a result of your notes?

External quality assurance

External quality assurance (EQA) relates to the monitoring of assessment and internal quality assurance (IQA) processes within a *centre* which has been approved by an awarding organisation (AO) to deliver and assess their qualifications. Any organisation can become an approved centre: for example colleges, charities, public, private, voluntary organisations and training providers, providing they meet the qualification and the AOs requirements. However, the EQA role is not just about monitoring, it's also about supporting the centre staff, and giving advice and guidance to help them get things right. At some point, you might have contact with an external quality assurer, perhaps during their visit, via a remote verification, on the telephone or by email. Please remember, an EQA is there to help and support you. If you have any questions, don't wait until the next planned visit, but keep in touch in the interim period. The EQA will also need to be notified of any staff or resource changes.

Your learners, when they successfully complete a qualification, will receive a certificate with the awarding organisation's name on, as well as the centre's name. Therefore, the EQA must ensure everything is in order, or their reputation as well as the centre's could be brought into disrepute.

External quality assurance must take place on behalf of an awarding organisation to ensure the learners who have been registered with them have received a quality service. It also seeks to ensure that assessment and internal quality assurance have been conducted in a consistent, safe and fair manner.

- **Consistent** – all staff are using similar assessment methods and making similar decisions across all learners. All learners have an equal chance of receiving an accurate assessment decision.

- **Safe** – the methods used to assess and internally quality assure are ethical, there is little chance of plagiarism by learners, the work can be confirmed as authentic, confidentially was taken into account, learning was not compromised, nor was the learner's experience or potential to achieve. (Safe in this context does not relate to health and safety but to the robustness and reliability of the assessment and IQA methods used.)

- **Fair** – the methods used are appropriate to all learners at the required level, and take into account any particular learner needs. Activities are fit for purpose, and planning, decisions and feedback are justifiable and equitable.

An EQA will need to follow the awarding organisation's guidelines as well as relevant regulations such as those issued by Ofqual. It is the regulator of qualifications, examinations and assessments in England, and vocational qualifications in Northern Ireland. Ofqual approves and regulates awarding organisations and the EQA will need to comply with its *General Conditions of Recognition* (2015). This document sets out certain conditions which awarding organisations must ensure their centres adhere to. Examples include managing conflicts of interest, identifying and managing risk, and dealing with malpractice.

Activity

Obtain a copy of the 2015 General Conditions of Recognition (just type these words in to an internet search engine if you can't obtain a hard copy) and have a look at the conditions. Make a note of how they will impact upon your role as an assessor. If you are currently assessing, you might like to discuss the content of the document with your colleagues.

There needs to be a system of monitoring the performance and decisions of assessors and internal quality assurers within a centre. If not, staff might make incorrect judgements, or pass a learner who hasn't met all the requirements, perhaps because they are biased towards them, or have made a mistake.

Example

Jeff had been assessing the Level 3 Work Based Horse Care and Management qualification for a number of years. The EQA was shortly due to visit and the IQA had asked him to help prepare for the visit. He first checked the last EQA report to make sure all the action points had been met. He then looked at the EQA visit plan to ensure everything that had been asked for would be available. This included obtaining the requested learners' work, copies of minutes of meetings, standardisation records, and an updated appeals' procedure. The EQA had also asked to see a feedback session between the IQA and Jeff, and to visit a learner in their workplace. With a bit of communication to the relevant people, Jeff was able to arrange all of this. The subsequent EQA visit went smoothly and no action points were given.

An EQA will complete a report which will identify aspects of good practice, as well as any relevant action and improvement points. Action points must be carried out by an agreed date, and relate to qualification and regulatory requirements. If they are not carried out, a sanction can be imposed upon the centre, for example, not allowing them to claim any certificates until the issues are resolved. Improvement points are matters which have been discussed to help a centre improve, but which wouldn't result in a sanction if not met. See Table 5.2 below.

Table 5.2 Examples of risk ratings and sanctions

Risk rating	Meaning	Sanctions
Low	The centre is complying with all awarding organisation and qualification requirements. There might be some minor issues that need addressing, in which case an appropriate action plan can be agreed with the centre.	Sanctions are not imposed on the centre and they can register and certificate their learners.
Medium	There is some non-compliance, for example, insufficient record keeping.	The centre can register their learners, but cannot claim certificates unless the external quality assurer carries out a further sample.
High	There are serious non-compliance issues, e.g. insufficient staff, no internal quality assurance system in place, or inaccurate data is maintained.	The centre cannot register any more learners or claim certificates for existing learners. High risk can also mean a centre having their approval status withdrawn from offering particular qualifications, if aspects are very serious.

Roles and responsibilities of an external quality assurer

The main role will be to maintain compliance on behalf of the awarding organisation and regulatory authorities.

This might include:

- advising and supporting centre staff on an ongoing basis (not just during visits)

- approving centres to offer qualifications

- communicating with centre staff and the awarding organisation on an ongoing basis

- completing a report of what was sampled, highlighting any action and improvement points, and judging whether the centre has a low, medium or high risk rating

- ensuring that a centre's policies, procedures, systems and resources meet awarding organisation, qualification and regulatory requirements

- ensuring that centre staff interpret, understand and consistently apply the correct standards and requirements

- ensuring that accuracy and consistency of assessment and internal quality assurance decisions

- ensuring that centre staff standardise their practice

- ensuring that learners are registered with the awarding organisation within the required timescale (learners who are not registered should not be sampled by the EQA)

- giving guidance to centre staff regarding the qualification content and requirements

- identifying issues and trends: for example, if all assessors are misinterpreting the same aspect of something

- keeping accurate, full and confidential records

- monitoring and auditing the full learner journey from commencement to completion: information, advice and guidance (IAG), recruitment, initial assessment, induction, training, formative and summative assessment, decision making, feedback, support for progression opportunities

- monitoring risk within a centre, for example when new standards are introduced, or if there is a high staff turnover

- observing assessment, feedback and IQA practice

- planning what will be monitored and when, and communicating this beforehand to all concerned within the awarding organisation's timescales

- recommending a sanction if there are problems

- releasing certification rights (known as *direct claims status*) when a centre is performing satisfactorily, or recommending removal of direct claims status if necessary

- sampling assessed and internally quality assured learners' work (and records) according to a planned strategy, and making decisions based on facts

- updating their own continuing professional development (CPD) regarding subject knowledge and EQA practice

- using technology where relevant: for example, sampling learners' evidence, assessment and IQA records remotely via an online learning program.

The EQA process

If a qualification is internally assessed and quality assured, external quality assurance must take place. This is to ensure and maintain compliance with the awarding organisation's and relevant regulatory bodies' requirements.

An external quality assurer will be appointed by an awarding organisation to monitor the activities of centres which offer their qualifications.

As a minimum, the external quality assurer should:

- plan what will be monitored, from whom and when (this could be during a visit to the centre or via a remote monitoring activity)

- meet with learners, assessors and IQAs

- observe assessor and internal quality assurers' performance

- sample assessment records, learners' work, assessment, IQA decisions and feedback

- provide feedback and guidance

- complete a report and recommend action and improvement points.

The external quality assurance cycle

Depending upon the subject, the EQA cycle will usually be followed as in Figure 5.2. The cycle will continue to ensure the assessment and IQA process is constantly monitored and improved if necessary. Records of all activities must be maintained throughout to satisfy the regulatory authorities and awarding organisation. The EQA cycle works in a similar way to the IQA cycle.

The EQA cycle involves the following aspects:

Identify the product or service – ascertaining what is to be externally quality assured and why. The criteria will need to be clear, i.e. units from a qualification (product) or aspects of the learner journey such as induction, initial assessment, tutorial reviews (service). External quality assurers might also carry out approval and advisory visits, as well as a monitoring visit or a remote monitoring activity to sample learners' work, assessment and IQA records.

Planning – devising a sample plan to arrange what will be monitored, from whom and when. Plan the dates to observe staff and talk to learners, and others involved, such as witnesses from the workplace. Information will need to be obtained from the centre staff to assist the planning process, and risks taken into account, such as staff turnover, knowledge and experience.

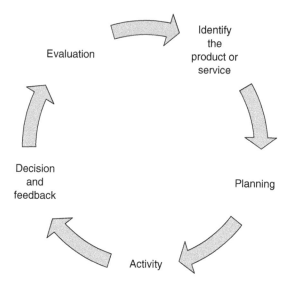

Figure 5.2 The external quality assurance (EQA) cycle

Activity – carrying out activities such as sampling assessment and IQA decisions and practice, sampling records and talking to learners and others. Centre staff should comply with the required assessment strategy for the qualification and be consistent in their role. Concerns, issues, trends, complaints and appeals should always be monitored.

The activities could be carried out during a visit to the centre or remotely (where documents are posted to the external quality assurer or accessed electronically), and should ensure quality and compliance of all aspects. Activities might also include approving centres to offer qualifications, and making decisions to release certification (known as *direct claims status*). Awarding organisations will give advice regarding the activities that should be carried out.

Decision and feedback – making a judgement as to whether the centre staff have performed satisfactorily, made valid and reliable decisions, and followed all required policies and procedures. Give developmental feedback as to what was good or what could be improved. Agree action and improvement points, if necessary, with appropriate target dates. Complete the awarding organisation's report and identify a risk rating of low, medium or high. See Table 5.2 on page 135 for examples.

Evaluation – reviewing the whole process to determine what is good practice, what could be improved or what could be done differently, and partaking in the awarding organisation's review, appraisal and standardisation processes.

The cycle will then begin again with an identification of what needs to be monitored and when. Throughout the cycle, standardisation of practice between external quality assurers should take place; this will help ensure the consistency and fairness of decisions and the support given to centres. This might be at formal meetings, or via online webinars or another appropriate method. Records of all activities must be maintained. All external quality assurers should maintain their continuing professional development (CPD) to ensure their own practice is current, and follow all relevant legal and organisational requirements.

Extension Activity

If you assess an accredited qualification, ask if you can see the most recent EQA report. Have a look at the comments which were made, and any supporting action or improvement points. Do you need to change anything you are doing as a result? You might like to discuss the content of the report with other assessors or your IQA.

Appeals, complaints and disputes

An *appeal* is usually about an assessment decision which a learner would like to be reconsidered. A *complaint* is likely to be about a situation or a person, and a *dispute* about a difference of opinion. Learners who appeal or complain should be able to do so without fear of recrimination. Confidentiality should be maintained where possible to ensure an impartial outcome, and the learner should feel protected throughout the full process. If anyone does make an appeal or complaint, this should not affect the way they are treated, and the outcome should not jeopardise their current or future achievements. The relevant persons should be informed of all situations which might lead to an appeal, complaint or dispute.

Assessment decisions should always be fair and ethical. If this happens, the number of appeals, complaints and disputes should be minimal.

- **Fair** – the assessment activity was appropriate to all learners at the required level, was inclusive, i.e. available to all, and differentiated for any particular needs. All learners had an equal chance of an accurate assessment decision.

- **Ethical** – the assessment process took into account confidentiality, integrity, safety, security and learner welfare.

Examples of appeals, complaints and disputes, and ways of avoiding them, could be part of the staff development process. The findings from all issues can be used as a basis to prevent similar situations occurring in the future. If you are assessing an accredited qualification, the awarding organisation will have advice about what to do in their qualification specification, which should be available on their website.

Activity

What do you think you can do to avoid any appeals, complaints and disputes regarding the subject you assess? Is this something you can communicate to your colleagues to ensure a consistent approach?

Appeals

At some point during the assessment process, a learner may wish to appeal against one of your decisions. Information regarding the appeals policy and procedure could be displayed on noticeboards, in a learner handbook, or be available via the organisation's intranet or VLE. Learners will need to know who they can go to, and that their issue will be followed up within a given timescale. The process will involve various stages and have deadlines, such as seven days to lodge an appeal, seven days for a response, and all stages should be documented. Usually, an appeals process is made up of four stages: assessor, internal quality assurer, manager, and external quality assurer (if applicable). The nature of the appeal can be used to inform future practice to prevent further appeals.

Example

Cheng had lodged a formal appeal straight to the internal quality assurer, Julia, regarding his assessor's decision for a unit from the Level 2 Customer Service qualification. He felt he should have passed as he had supplied all the required evidence. Julia spoke to the assessor and reviewed Cheng's evidence. It transpired that the assessor was correct in asking for a further piece of evidence. Julia spoke to Cheng and explained that four pieces of evidence were required and he had only submitted three. He accepted Julia's decision and agreed to supply a further piece of evidence. Cheng then retracted his appeal and wished he had followed the correct procedure by speaking to his assessor first.

Some organisations will provide an appeals pro-forma for learners to complete, which ensures all the required details are obtained, or encourage an informal discussion with the assessor first. Statistics should be maintained regarding all appeals and complaints; these will help your organisation when reviewing its policies and procedures, and should be provided to relevant external inspectors if requested.

Having a climate of respect and honesty can lead to issues being dealt with informally, rather than procedures having to be followed, which can be upsetting for all parties concerned.

Complaints

A complaint might occur from a learner, for example if an assessor has lost their work, or it has not been returned to them on time. The learner might complain verbally to the assessor or IQA first but then put in a formal complaint if they are not satisfied with the response. As with appeals, there should be a policy and procedure for complaints, with which you and your learners are familiar.

If you are concerned that a learner might make a complaint against you, talk to your supervisor and keep records of the situation. Take care not to become too informal with your learners, or have friendly chats when no one else is around which could be misinterpreted.

Disputes

A dispute might occur, for example if you assess a piece of work from a learner and think that they have plagiarised one aspect or all of it from another source. You would need to check this very carefully first. It might be that they have used a quote in a piece of academic writing, but omitted to reference it. In this case, it would not have been intentional and you can give feedback to your learner about the importance of referencing. It might be that they need further training how to do this. There are specialist programs and software available which can be used to check for plagiarism. The learners' electronic work can be submitted to the program and scanned to determine how much of it has occurred elsewhere. If your learner has plagiarised something deliberately, you will need to deal with them carefully, otherwise they may start a dispute which could get out of control. You might find it best to discuss your concerns with another assessor, or someone else, before you confront your learner. Always remain factual and calm; getting angry will not help the situation.

As with appeals and complaints, there should be a policy and procedure for disputes with which you and your learners are familiar.

Extension Activity

Locate your organisation's policies and procedures for appeals, complaints and disputes. Read them to make sure you are familiar with the content and what to do if a situation arises. If you are not assessing an accredited qualification, find out what your organisation expects you to do. If your qualification is accredited, find out what relevant information the awarding organisation provides, and how they would get involved if necessary.

Summary

Having your assessment activities quality assured, and taking part in standardisation events, will help ensure that you are being fair and accurate with your decisions and giving consistent support to your learners. Understanding a little about appeals, complaints and disputes might prevent them from occurring.

You might like to carry out further research by accessing the books and websites listed at the end of this chapter.

This chapter has covered the following topics:

- Standardising practice

- Internal quality assurance

- External quality assurance

- Appeals, complaints and disputes

References and further information

Ofqual (2009) *Authenticity – A Guide for Teachers*. Coventry: Ofqual.

Ofqual (2015) *General Conditions of Recognition*. Coventry: Ofqual.

Pontin, K. (2012) *Practical Guide to Quality Assurance*. London: City & Guilds.

Read, H. (2012) *The Best Quality Assurer's Guide*. Bideford: Read On Publications.

Wilson, L. A. (2012) *Practical Teaching: A Guide to Assessment and Quality Assurance*. Andover: Cengage Learning.

Wood, J. and Dickinson, J. (2011) *Quality Assurance and Evaluation in the Lifelong Learning Sector*. Exeter: Learning Matters.

Websites

Ofqual *General Conditions of Recognition* (2015) – **http://tinyurl.com/qfg3pum**

Plagiarism – **www.plagiarism.org** and **www.plagiarismadvice.org**

6 EVALUATION AND CONTINUING PROFESSIONAL DEVELOPMENT

Introduction

Evaluation is a quality assurance tool which enables you to obtain feedback in order to make improvements. Feedback can be from various people, such as the learner, their employer (if applicable) and support staff. This should relate to the products and services used throughout your learner's experience with you. The product is the programme, qualification or set of standards the learner is working towards. Services include everything that supports the learning and assessment experience.

This chapter will explore the evaluation process. It will also give you some ideas regarding your own continuing professional development to enable you to keep up to date with developments in your subject area and sector.

This chapter will cover the following topics:

- Programme evaluation
- Learner feedback
- Self-evaluation
- Continuing professional development

Programme evaluation

Whichever type of programme, qualification or set of standards you assess, no matter when or where, it's important to evaluate everything you have been involved with. This is to help make improvements not only to the programme, but for yourself and your current, and future learners. Programme evaluation focuses on the product (qualification or set of standards) which the learners are working towards.

You could obtain information, data and statistics such as retention, achievement, destination and progression. This information might be compiled by another department or it might be from a record you have maintained yourself. If you start a programme with 15 learners and only nine achieved at the end, then you need to find out why. It could be that the learners' needs were not met, they were on the wrong programme, or they left by personal choice. When analysing data regarding your programme and learners, you may need to compare this with national averages (if available). The Skills Funding Agency (SFA) issue qualification success rates (QSR) which are available via their website.

The findings and results from programme evaluations should feed into an overall quality report for the organisation. This is sometimes known as a self-assessment report (SAR) and might be a requirement if your organisation receives funding for learners.

The following list gives some examples of what can be evaluated, with a view to improving the programme:

- action plans and assessment plans

- assessment types and methods

- communication between assessors and others

- data, such as retention, achievement, destination and progression

- feedback to learners

- formative assessment activities

- initial and diagnostic assessment activities

- learner progression and destinations

- learner reviews and tutorials

- record keeping

- team meetings

- test results and grades

- standardisation activities

- summative assessment activities

- use of questions for assessment and during feedback

- validity and reliability of assessment methods, activities and decisions

- ways in which assessment activities are differentiated to meet any particular learner needs.

The methods you employ to gain feedback can include using *questionnaires and surveys* with anyone who has an interest in the programme and the learner. These can be carried out in a variety of ways, for example completed electronically or manually, anonymously or not. When you are considering what questions to ask and to whom, you need to think how to word them. This will enable you to obtain the information you need at the time, to evaluate the programme and recommend improvements.

You could decide to use a mixture of open and closed questions. Open questions always require a full response and give you *qualitative* data to work with, i.e. quality feedback. Closed questions elicit only a 'yes' or 'no' answer and give you *quantitative* data, i.e. you can add up the quantity (number) of responses. If you use a closed question, you could follow this up with an open question to enable you to obtain further quality information. The response might take longer for you to read and analyse, but you will have something more substantial to help with the evaluation process.

The example below gives a few closed questions, to gain quantitative data, which are then followed by open questions to gain qualitative data. These questions are to be used in a questionnaire to an employer of an apprentice who is attending a training organisation one day a week.

Example

1. **Does a Monday suit your organisation for your apprentice to attend day release sessions? Yes/No**

   If no, what day would be preferable and why?

2. **Does your apprentice tell you what they learn during their day release sessions? Yes/No**

   If yes, does this help inform their job role?

   If no, how could communication be improved?

3. **Are the subjects your apprentice is studying relevant to their job role? Yes/No**

   If no, what subjects would be more relevant and why?

Questions can be written in different ways in order to gain different types of responses. For example, a closed question could be followed by a response scale of 1 to 5 for respondents to circle (1 being no or low, 5 being yes or high). However, these scales only give you quantitative data to work with. If you want to know *why* an option has been chosen, you will need to ask further questions to obtain qualitative information. The following example gives different ways a question could be given to learners at the end of their programme.

Example

Did the programme fulfil your expectations? 1 2 3 4 5

Instead of numbers, you could use smiley faces for learners to circle. For example:

Did the programme fulfil your expectations? ☺ ☺ ☹

However, the tendency might be to choose number 3 or ☺ as they are in the middle. Removing one makes the response more definitive; for example:

Did the programme fulfil your expectations? 1 2 3 4

Or:

Did the programme fulfil your expectations? ☺ ☹

Having fewer options can help gain a more realistic response.

The type of programme you assess will influence the questions you ask. However, it could be that questionnaires and surveys are already in place and you just have to issue them to learners. You might be required to analyse the responses yourself, or another member of staff might do this, or they might be automatically analysed if completed electronically.

You could evaluate whether the assessment types and methods you use with your learners are working or not. There might be trends which need addressing, such as all learners not passing a particular aspect. This could be due to the wrong assessment method used, or a misunderstanding of what was expected. You will need to ensure the activities you used to assess skills, knowledge and understanding are valid and reliable, and that you only assess what you are meant to assess. You will also need to ask yourself if you assessed fairly and ethically, or if you had a favourite learner to whom you gave more attention, or were lenient with for any reason.

Evaluate a recent assessment activity you have used with your learner/s. How successful was it and why? Would you need to make any changes to the programme as a result? If so, what would they be and what impact would they have?

Feedback from your learners might impact upon the programme by enlightening you in other aspects; for example, the types of questions used in an assignment might have been too complex, some activities might not have been challenging enough, or a multiple-choice test confused a learner who has dyslexia as they mistook a 'b' for a 'd'.

Feedback from learners can help standardise the practice of assessors by ensuring the activities used are valid and reliable, and the types and methods of assessment are safe, fair and ethical. All feedback should be analysed and a report compiled which shows the results and recommendations. These should then be acted upon and followed up. There's no point carrying out a survey just for a survey's sake. Something should be done with the results which will lead to improvements. Keeping records and audit trails should help you identify situations and respond to them, hopefully in a proactive rather than reactive way.

Feedback from others

Besides learners, there are other people who will be able to give you feedback to help you evaluate the programme. These can include:

- inspectors

- internal and external quality assurers

- parents and carers of young and/or vulnerable learners

- support staff

- the learner's supervisor, employer and witnesses (if assessment is in the workplace)

- your line manager or supervisor

- your peers and colleagues.

Inspectors

It could be that inspectors from external agencies will need to visit the organisation where your learners are based, for example those regarding health, safety, security or food hygiene. They might be able to give you feedback which should help to improve the way the programme is delivered and assessed.

Internal and external quality assurers

There might be a quality assurance process in place to ensure that you are assessing in a fair and accurate way. If so, you should receive feedback from your internal quality assurer regarding what you have done well, and what can be improved and how.

If you are assessing towards an accredited qualification, there will be an external quality assurer who will monitor the programme to ensure quality and compliance.

Some of these people might observe you assessing a learner at some time. You will need to be prepared and have your assessment plans, learner details and individual progress and achievement records available. Your observer might also talk to your learner about the programme. If you are observed assessing a learner in the workplace, you should inform the learner and their employer in advance. It might not be appropriate for some-one else to be in the learner's workplace, or special arrangements might need to be made. For example, the observer might need personal protective equipment (PPE), be security cleared, or need directions if they are not travelling with you. Please see Chapter 5 for more information regarding quality assurance.

Parents and carers of young and/or vulnerable learners

Where possible, talk to the parents and carers of young and/or vulnerable learners. They, along with the learners, should be able to give you valuable feedback regarding anything which could support them whilst taking the programme.

Support staff

There should be support staff available to help with the programme, giving support to you and/or your learners. Depending upon the type of employment contract you have, you will need to find out who these people are, how they can support the programme, and how you can obtain feedback from them. You might not think gaining feedback from them would help improve the programme; however, they might notice things you haven't which could help the way you do things. Administrative staff might be able to give you data regarding numbers of applicants, starters and leavers. They might also keep records of destinations of learners when they leave, and funding information based on achievements. Support staff might include:

- administrators

- careers staff

- caretakers

- cleaners

- exam officers

- information, advice and guidance staff (IAG)

- learning and learner support staff

- learning resource centre (LRC) staff

- receptionists.

The learner's supervisor, employer and witnesses (if assessment is in the workplace)
If you assess in the workplace, you would find it really beneficial to obtain feedback from your learner's supervisor, their employer and any staff who give witness testimonies or carry out training. They work closely with your learner and will be able to give you valuable advice regarding how the programme is, or is not, supporting learning and progression.

Your line manager or supervisor
Your role might involve you partaking in an appraisal or review process. As a result, you will receive feedback which you can use to help you develop as an assessor, as well as feedback regarding the way the programme is assessed. You should be notified of the date and time, and you might find it useful to prepare some questions in advance. If you don't partake in a formal appraisal or review, you can always ask for informal feedback.

Your peers and colleagues
Feedback from peers and colleagues could be informal, for example discussions about how the programme is progressing, or formal, as part of a meeting or a peer observation process.

There will be different ways of obtaining feedback from each of those mentioned. You will need to find out what your involvement would be regarding gaining feedback, how you would go about it and what you would do with the responses.

Extension Activity

Find out what systems are in place at your organisation regarding programme evaluation. Look at the bullet list on pages 146–7 of people you can gain feedback from, and add any others you can think of. Consider who you would involve and why. Ask someone if you can see a previous questionnaire and the resulting analysis, report and recommendations.

Learner feedback

Obtaining feedback from learners will help you improve their learning experience. Your learners should have the opportunity to evaluate the services they receive, perhaps by completing a questionnaire or survey or taking part in a focus discussion group.

The services learners receive relate to all the aspects which underpin and support their experiences. Listed opposite are some examples. Not all will be applicable, depending upon the context of learning and assessment. The experience and support you give your learners as their assessor is also included.

Learners could give feedback on the following services:

- application and interview process
- assessment experience and support
- career and progression opportunities
- catering and refreshments
- childcare
- financial support
- health and welfare advice
- information, advice and guidance
- learning support such as help with dyslexia, maths and English
- leisure facilities
- library and learning resource facilities
- parking and smoking areas
- transport.

If your organisation is aiming to be classed as *outstanding* by Ofsted, then it will be keen on the *learner voice*. This is the involvement of learners in shaping the learning opportunities that are available to them. It means involving and supporting them to act as partners with policy-makers, providers, practitioners and other agencies. Learner voice initiatives seek to include the learner by enabling them to express their concerns, needs and views in a safe way. This could be by the use of anonymous questionnaires, focus groups or online surveys. Organisations should respond appropriately to the issues that are raised, and give feedback regarding the developments and changes that result. This places the learner at the centre of policy and practice. The learner voice should be incorporated into the programme review process, covered in the previous section of this chapter.

Activity

Think about and list the different ways you could obtain feedback from your learners, besides using a questionnaire or survey.

Ways of obtaining feedback from learners

When obtaining feedback from learners, you should choose a method which is appropriate to them, and the information you wish to acquire. Feedback can be obtained when you are with your learners (individually or in groups) or via another method, for example:

- comment cards

- email

- feedback forms

- focus groups

- interview or discussion: one-to-one or in groups

- online: electronic surveys, video calls, polls or customer reviews

- paper-based surveys

- postal questionnaires

- social media communications and discussion forums

- suggestion boxes

- telephone/teleconference

- webinar or online chat.

Whichever method you decide to use, it should be appropriate to your learners, and follow your organisation's procedures. There's no point creating and issuing a questionnaire for the sake of it; all feedback you request should lead to improvements and developments for everyone concerned. If your role involves obtaining feedback, you might like to research the methods in the above bullet list further.

Talking to your learners informally can help you realise how successful the learning process has been. This can be carried out during tutorial reviews, at breaktimes, or before or after an assessment activity. Your learners are the best judges of whether they are getting what they feel they need. If given the opportunity, they may give you more feedback in an informal situation. You could ask your learners directly, after an assessment activity, how they felt the process went. However, while some learners might feel confident enough to tell you, others might not.

Example

Elias was assessing his workplace learners for the Level 2 Warehousing and Storage qualification. As he worked at the same organisation as his learners, he was familiar with all the services available to support them at work. However, he wanted to find out what the services were like at their day release centre. He decided to speak to his learners as a group, but no one was forthcoming in front of their peers. He then designed a short survey for them to complete anonymously online. To his surprise, he received a lot of feedback, most of which was complimentary. He was able to discuss the other issues with the training centre to ensure that they were resolved.

There are online programs available which can be used to obtain feedback anonymously, or your organisation might have this facility as part of their intranet or virtual learning environment (VLE). If a learner can give anonymous feedback, they might give more information than if they were talking directly to you.

Social media, in the right context and used appropriately, could also be used to obtain feedback. However, this would probably not be anonymous if the learner had to use their online account.

Questionnaires and online surveys

When issuing questionnaires or using surveys (whether electronically or manually), decide first whether you want the responses to be anonymous or not. Always give a date for completion and return, otherwise people may take their time or forget. The response rate is not usually high when people are left to complete them in their own time. Therefore, if you can allow time when you are with your learners, you should receive a higher response. If you are not watching over your learners completing it, then it will remain anonymous.

When designing your questionnaire or survey, think about the type of questions you want to ask, how clearly they are written, and whether they are at the right level for the learner. This will help you to obtain the information you need in an inclusive way. You could use closed questions such as:

- Were the assessment approaches suitable? Yes/No

or open questions such as:

- How did you find the assessment approaches?

The latter is better as you should gain more information from an open question. However, it might not be appropriate for a lower-level learner if they are not able to elaborate on the different assessment approaches. You might be available at the time to help them with their answer, but that might influence what they would like to say.

If you are likely to be with your learners for a long-term programme, such as a year, it's best to gain feedback early on, part way through, and towards the end (for example, once a term during an academic year). This will enable you to act upon feedback as necessary while the learners are still with you.

Whatever you decide to ask, make sure you keep your questions simple: don't ask two questions in one sentence or use complicated jargon, allow space for written responses, give a date for completion, and thank your learners for their contributions.

You could carry out a small sample survey with just a few learners to see how it works first. This is called a *pilot* and allows you to make any changes for the full survey if necessary.

Always analyse the responses and inform your learners how their contributions have led to changes and the resulting improvements.

Create a few questions that you could use with your own learners to gain feedback. Consider what information you would like to know and why, and then devise your questions carefully (electronically or manually).

If possible, use the questions with your learners (anonymously or not), analyse the responses and consider the changes you would make as a result. If you can, implement the changes.

Self-evaluation

Self-evaluation will help you learn about yourself and what you could improve, for example how you react to different situations or learners, how patient you are and what skills you may need to develop. You might also decide as a result that you need further training perhaps to improve your subject knowledge and/or English and maths skills.

Self-evaluation can take place at any time, just by asking yourself what went well and what could be improved. For example, 'How do I know that my learner understood the feedback I gave them?' If you can't answer this, you will need to make some changes to the way you give feedback. Perhaps begin by asking your learner a question to check their understanding.

Reflection

Reflection is about becoming more self-aware, which should give you increased confidence and improve the links between the theory and practice of assessment. It is often just your thoughts, which can be positive or negative, but can also take into account any feedback you have received. It is useful to keep a learning journal or a diary to note anything important; you can then refer to this when planning your future development or preparing for assessments.

Activity

Start keeping a diary, either in note form or electronically, and document the next few assessment activities you carry out. How did you manage the process to ensure the assessment activity was successful, and how did you know learning had taken place?

Theories of reflection

A straightforward method of reflection is to have the experience, then describe it, analyse it and revise it (EDAR). This method incorporates the *who, what, when, where, why* and *how* approach (WWWWWH), and should help you consider ways of changing and/or improving.

Experience → Describe → Analyse → Revise (EDAR)

- **E**xperience – a significant event or incident you would like to change or improve.

- **D**escribe – aspects such as who was involved, what happened, when it happened and where it happened.

- **A**nalyse – consider the experience more deeply and ask yourself how it happened and why it happened.

- **R**evise – think about how you would do it differently if it happened again and then try this out if you have the opportunity.

Self-reflection should become a part of your everyday activities, enabling you to analyse and focus on things in greater detail. All reflection should lead to an improvement in practice; however, there may be events you would not want to change or improve as you felt they went well. If this is the case, reflect as to why they went well and use these methods again. If you are not able to write a reflective learning journal, mentally run through the EDAR points in your head when you have time. As you become more experienced at reflective practice, you will see how you can improve and develop further.

There are various theories regarding reflection. Schön (1983) suggests two methods:

- reflection in action

- reflection on action.

Reflection *in* action happens at the time of the incident, is often unconscious, is proactive and allows immediate changes to take place.

Example

Roisin was about to assess a group of adults attending college as part of a day release Business Studies programme. She had designed an assignment for them to complete but had underestimated how fast they would work through it. As they were progressing, she quickly devised some extra activities. She then issued them to the group when they completed the assignment. She was able to reflect immediately, to ensure the learners were further challenged and kept occupied. Roisin therefore carried out reflection in action. If she had not done anything, her learners would have been left with nothing productive to do. Roisin would have had to reflect on action after the event about what she would do if the situation arose again.

Reflection *on* action takes place after the incident; it is a more conscious process and is reactive. This allows you time to think about the incident, consider a different approach, or to talk to others about it before making changes. However, it will not allow you to deal with a situation as it occurs, as in the previous example.

Brookfield (1995) identified the importance of being critical when reflecting. He advocated four points of view when looking at your practice, which he called critical lenses. These lenses are from the point of view of:

- the teacher (and/or assessor)

- the learner

- colleagues

- theories and literature.

Using these points makes the reflection critical: first, by looking at it from your own point of view as a teacher (and/or assessor); second, finding out how your learner perceived your actions and what they liked and disliked; third, taking into consideration the view of your colleagues, such as your peers or mentor. This enables you to have a critical conversation about your actions which might highlight things you hadn't considered. Fourth, you should link your reflections to theories and literature, comparing your own ideas with others' published work.

Kolb (1984) proposed a four-stage continuous learning process. His theory suggests that without reflection, people would continue to make mistakes. When you are assessing, you may make mistakes; you should therefore consider why they happened and what you would do differently next time, putting your plans into practice when you have the opportunity.

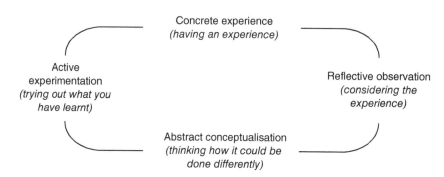

Concrete experience
(having an experience)

Active experimentation
(trying out what you have learnt)

Reflective observation
(considering the experience)

Abstract conceptualisation
(thinking how it could be done differently)

Figure 6.1 Kolb's four-stage model of learning

Kolb's model suggests that the cycle can be started at any stage; that reflection is as important as the experience; and that once the cycle is started it should be followed through all the stages for it to be effective.

What works with one learner or group might not work well with others, perhaps due to their learning preferences or other influences. Don't change something for the sake of it; if it works, hopefully it will continue to work.

Reflect upon the next assessment activity you carry out. Use EDAR, Schön, Brookfield or Kolb's model to help you evaluate what went well, and what didn't. Identify areas for improvement and/or development. Do you need any further training and/or support? If so, how will you go about obtaining it?

Continuing professional development

Continuing professional development (CPD) can be anything you do which helps you improve your practice. It shows you are a committed professional and it should help improve your skills, knowledge and understanding. CPD should relate to your job role as well as to the subjects you assess, and can be based on the results of evaluation and feedback. You should reflect on the activities you carry out so that they have a positive impact upon your development and role. There are constant changes in education; therefore it is crucial to keep up to date and embrace them. Examples include changes to the qualifications or standards you assess, and changes to policies and practices within your organisation, regulatory requirements and government initiatives. It's useful to add relevant CPD to your curriculum vitae, particularly if you are applying for a job or promotion.

CPD can be formal or informal, planned well in advance or be opportunistic, but it should have a real impact upon your role and lead to an improvement in your practice. CPD is more than just attending events or carrying out research; it is also about using reflection regarding your experiences which results in your improvement and/or development as an assessor.

Your organisation might have a strategy for CPD which will prioritise activities they consider are important to improving standards, and may or may not provide any funding for them. However, you can partake in lots of activities which cost very little. For example, you could observe colleagues, visit organisations (if you have apprentice learners you might like to find out about the areas they work in), research websites, and read journals and text books.

Look at the following list and decide which of the activities would be relevant to you. What other activities could you carry out which would contribute towards your CPD?

Opportunities for professional development include:

- attending relevant events and training programmes
- attending meetings
- e-learning and online activities

- evaluating feedback from peers, learners and others
- formally reflecting on experiences and documenting how it has improved practice
- improving your own skills, such as English, maths and ICT
- keeping up to date with relevant legislation
- membership of professional associations or committees
- observing colleagues
- reading text books and journals
- researching developments or changes to your subject as well as assessment practice
- secondments
- self-reflection
- shadowing colleagues
- standardisation activities
- studying for relevant qualifications
- subscribing to and reading relevant journals and websites
- using social media to follow/inform others of relevant and current information
- visiting other organisations
- voluntary work
- work experience placements
- writing or reviewing books and articles.

It's a good idea to maintain a record of all CPD undertaken, to prove you are remaining current with your assessment role and your subject specialism. You could keep a manual record, such as the one shown in Table 6.1, or an electronic record, perhaps as a spreadsheet, or by using specialist software.

Using a reference number for each activity enables you to cross-reference the activities to your documentation; for example, number 1 could refer to minutes of meetings, number 2 could be a certificate, number 3 a record of achievement. Adding the reference number to the relevant documents also enables you to locate them when necessary. Besides keeping your CPD record up to date, you should write a more detailed reflection of what you learnt and how it impacted upon your job role.

You might participate in an appraisal or performance review system at some time in your organisation. This is a valuable opportunity to discuss your progress, development and any training and/or support you may need. Having the support of your organisation will help you decide what is relevant to your development as an assessor, and towards your job role. An appraisal or an informal discussion is also a chance to reflect upon your achievements and successes. Always keep a copy of any documentation relating to your training and CPD, as you may need to provide this to funding bodies, awarding organisations or regulatory bodies if requested.

Table 6.1 Example CPD record

Continuing professional development record					
Name: Abbi Cross			Organisation: Excellence Training		
Date	Activity and venue	Duration	Justification towards assessment role and subject specialism	Action required	Ref. no.
6 Jan	Attendance at standardisation event. Four assessors, myself and the IQA discussed how we interpreted the requirements of units 101, 102 and 103 and reassessed each other's decisions.	3 hrs	Standardised assessment practice to ensure I am assessing the Level 3 Certificate in Hospitality & Catering in the same way as the other assessors.	Units 104 and 105 to be standardised next time. Obtain copies of my assessment records for the next meeting.	1
10 Feb	Attendance at a First Aid training day.	6 hrs	To ensure I am current with First Aid in case someone has an accident.	–	2
20 Mar	Attendance at staff training event for assessors. All assessors were able to get together and discuss the types of records we use. We were also given updates regarding policies and procedures.	3 hrs	Ensured I am up to date with policies and procedures regarding assessment practice. Also helped me realise I had been completing a form in a different way from other assessors.	Be consistent with how I complete my records. Make a list of improvements I would recommend prior to the next event.	3

The practice of assessment has been recognised as a professional activity by the granting of Chartered status to the Institute of Educational Assessors (CIEA). Their aim is to improve the quality of assessment in schools and colleges by working with educational assessors to develop their knowledge, understanding and capability in all aspects of educational testing and assessment. You can access their standards by visiting their website (www.ciea.org.uk).

Keeping up to date

The following websites are useful to gain up-to-date information regarding developments in the further education and skills sector. Most of them enable you to register for electronic updates.

Department for Business, Innovation and Skills – **www.bis.gov.uk**

Department for Education – **www.gov.uk/government/organisations/department-for-education**

Education and Training Foundation – **www.et-foundation.co.uk**

Equality and Diversity Forum – **www.edf.org.uk**

FE News – **www.fenews.co.uk**

FE Week – **www.feweek.co.uk**

Government updates: Education and Learning – **www.gov.uk/browse/education**

National Institute of Adult Continuing Education – **www.niace.org.uk**

Ofqual – **www.ofqual.gov.uk**

Ofsted – **www.ofsted.gov.uk**

Teacher Educator UK – **https://teachereducatoruk.wikispaces.com**

Times Educational Supplement online – **www.tes.co.uk**

UKFEChat – **www.ukfechat.com**

You could join free social network sites such as LinkedIn, which is a professional networking site (www.linkedin.co.uk). Here you will find groups you can join specifically aimed at your specialist subject. You can post questions and respond to queries, and join in regular discussions.

Ann Gravells regularly uses Twitter to inform her followers of what's happening in the further education and skills sector. You can follow her at www.twitter.com by searching for @AnnGravells. She also uses other social media such as LinkedIn, Facebook and Google+.

Following relevant people or organisations via social media will enable you to keep up to date with their posts.

Extension Activity

Decide on a system for documenting your CPD if you don't already have one. You could use a form as in Table 6.1, or you could design your own. Add some recent activities to it and reflect upon each activity you have carried out, and how it has impacted upon your role as an assessor. If you have time, look at the websites listed in the previous bullet list and subscribe for updates from relevant ones or your awarding organisation (if applicable).

Summary

Reflecting upon your own assessment practice, taking account of feedback from learners, colleagues and others, and maintaining your professional development should enable you to become a more effective assessor.

You might like to carry out further research by accessing the books and websites listed at the end of this chapter.

This chapter has covered the following topics:

- Programme evaluation

- Learner feedback

- Self-evaluation

- Continuing professional development

References and further information

Brookfield, S. (1995) *Becoming a Critically Reflective Teacher*. San Francisco: Jossey-Bass.

Denscombe, M. (2014) *The Good Research Guide*, Maidenhead: Open University Press.

Hill, C. (2008) *Teaching with E-learning*. Exeter: Learning Matters.

Kolb, D. A. (1984) *Experiential Learning: Experience as the Source for Learning and Development*. New Jersey: Prentice-Hall.

Roffey-Barentsen, J. and Malthouse, R. (2013) *Reflective Practice in Education and Training* (2nd edn). Exeter: Learning Matters.

Rushton, I. and Suter, M. (2012) *Reflective Practice for Teaching in Lifelong Learning*. Maidenhead: Open University Press.

Scales, P. et al. (2011) *Continuing Professional Development in the Lifelong Learning Sector*. Maidenhead: Open University Press.

Schön, D. (1983) *The Reflective Practitioner*. San Francisco: Jossey-Bass.

Sellars, M. (2014) *Reflective Practice for Teachers*. London: SAGE

Wood, J. and Dickinson, J. (2011) *Quality Assurance and Evaluation in the Lifelong Learning Sector*. Exeter: Learning Matters.

Websites

Association for Achievement and Improvement through Assessment (AAIA) – **www.aaia.org.uk**

Chartered Institute of Educational Assessors – **www.ciea.org.uk**

Facebook – **www.facebook.com**

Google+ – **www.google.com**

LinkedIn – **www.linkedin.com**

Questionnaire design – **www.wireuk.org/ten-steps-towards-designing-a-questionnaire.html**

Self-evaluation – **www2.warwick.ac.uk/services/ldc/resource/evaluation/tools/self/**

Skills Funding Agency – **www.gov.uk/government/organisations/skills-funding-agency**

Twitter – **www.twitter.com**

Online surveys – **www.surveymonkey.com** and **www.smartsurvey.co.uk**

Abbreviations and Acronyms

AAIA	Association for Achievement and Improvement through Assessment
ACL	Adult and Community Learning
ADD	Attention Deficit Disorder
ADHD	Attention Deficit and Hyperactivity Disorder
ADS	Adult Dyslexia Support
AELP	Association of Employment and Learning Providers
AI	Awarding Institution
AO	Awarding Organisation
AoC	Association of Colleges
ASD	Autism Spectrum Disorder
ATL	Association of Teachers and Lecturers
BEd	Bachelor of Education
BIS	Department for Business, Innovation and Skills
BKSB	Basic Key Skills Builder
BYOD	Bring Your Own Device
CCEA	Council for the Curriculum, Examinations and Assessment (Northern Ireland)
CETT	Centre for Excellence in Teacher Training
Cert Ed	Certificate in Education
CIEA	Chartered Institute for Educational Assessors
CIF	Common Inspection Framework
CL	Community Learning
CLA	Copyright Licensing Authority
COSHH	Control of Substances Hazardous to Health

CPD	Continuing Professional Development
CQFW	Credit and Qualification Framework for Wales
CRB	Criminal Records Bureau (now part of DBS)
DBS	Disclosure and Barring Service
DCELLS	Department for Children, Education, Lifelong Learning and Skills (Wales)
DfE	Department for Education
DSO	Designated Safeguarding Officer
E&D	Equality and Diversity
EBD	Emotional and Behavioural Difficulties
ECDL	European Computer Driving Licence
EDAR	Experience, Describe, Analyse, Revise
EDIP	Explain, Demonstrate, Imitate, Practise
EI	Emotional Intelligence
EHRC	Equality and Human Rights Commission
ESOL	English for Speakers of Other Languages
ETF	Education and Training Foundation
EQA	External Quality Assurance/Assurer
FAQ	Frequently Asked Questions
FE	Further Education
FELTAG	Further Education Learning Technology Action Group
FHE	Further and Higher Education
GCSE	General Certificate of Secondary Education
GLH	Guided Learning Hours
H&S	Health and Safety
HEA	Higher Education Academy
HEI	Higher Education Institution
IAG	Information, Advice and Guidance
IAP	Individual Action Plan
ICT	Information and Communication Technology
IfL	Institute for Learning (no longer operational)
IIP	Investors In People

ILA	Individual Learning Account
ILM	Institute for Leadership and Management
ILP	Individual Learning Plan
ILT	Information and Learning Technology
IT	Information Technology
ITE	Initial Teacher Education
ITOL	Institute of Training and Occupational Learning
ITP	Independent Training Provider
ISA	Independent Safeguarding Authority (now part of DBS)
ITT	Initial Teacher/Trainer Training
IQ	Intelligence Quotient
IQA	Internal Quality Assurance/Assurer
IWB	Interactive Whiteboard
LA	Local Authority
LAR	Learner Achievement Record
LDD	Learning Difficulties and/or Disabilities
LLUK	Lifelong Learning UK (no longer operational)
LRC	Learning Resource Centre
LSA	Learner (or Learning) Support Assistant
LSIS	Learning and Skills Improvement Service (no longer operational)
LSCB	Local Safeguarding Children Board
MLD	Moderate Learning Difficulties
MOOCs	Massive Open Online Courses
NEET	Not in Education, Employment or Training
NIACE	National Institute of Adult Continuing Education
NLH	Notional Learning Hours
NLP	Neuro Linguistic Programming
NOS	National Occupational Standards
NQT	Newly Qualified Teacher
NRDC	National Research and Development Centre for adult literacy and numeracy
NTA	Non-teaching Assistant

NVQ	National Vocational Qualification
OER	Open Education Resources
Ofqual	Office of Qualifications and Examinations Regulation
Ofsted	Office for Standards in Education, Children's Services and Skills
OU	Open University
PAT	Portable Appliance Testing
PCET	Post Compulsory Education and Training
PDBW	Personal Development, Behaviour and Welfare
PGCE	Post Graduate Certificate in Education
PLTS	Personal Learning and Thinking Skills
POCA	Protection of Children Act (1999)
PPE	Personal Protective Equipment
PPP	Pose, Pause, Pick
PSHE	Personal, Social and Health Education
QCF	Qualifications and Credit Framework (replaced by RQF)
QSR	Qualification Success Rates
QTLS	Qualified Teacher Learning and Skills (further education and skills)
QTS	Qualified Teacher Status (schools)
RARPA	Recognising and Recording Progress and Achievement in non-accredited learning
RQF	Regulated Qualifications Framework
RIDDOR	Reporting of Injuries, Diseases and Dangerous Occurrences Regulations
RLJ	Reflective Learning Journal
RPL	Recognition of Prior Learning
RWE	Realistic Working Environment
SAR	Self-Assessment Report
SARA	Shock, Anger, Resistance, Acceptance
SET	Society for Education and Training
SCN	Scottish Candidate Number
SCQF	Scottish Credit and Qualifications Framework
SfA	Skills Funding Agency

SL	Student Loan
SLC	Subject Learning Coach
SMART	Specific, Measurable, Achievable, Relevant and Timebound
SoW	Scheme of Work
SP	Session Plan
SSB	Standard Setting Body
SSC	Sector Skills Council
SWOT	Strengths, Weaknesses, Opportunities and Threats
T&L	Teaching and Learning
TAQA	Training, Assessment and Quality Assurance
TNA	Training Needs Analysis
TQT	Total Qualification Time
UCU	University and College Union
ULN	Unique Learner Number
VACSR	Valid, Authentic, Current, Sufficient, Reliable
VARK	Visual, Aural, Read/write, Kinaesthetic
VET	Vocational Education and Training
VB	Vetting and Barring
VLE	Virtual Learning Environment
WBL	Work Based Learning
WEA	Workers' Educational Association
WWWWWH	Who, What, When, Where, Why and How

INDEX

Added to a page number 'f' denotes a figure and 't' denotes a table.